Contents

< TITLE PAGE: BICYCLE SCENE
<< FULL PAGE: BROUWERSGRACHT

INTRODUCTION TO

Amsterdam

There's nowhere quite like Amsterdam. You could be sitting nursing a drink outside one of its cafés, chugging by boat along its canals, or riding its ringing trams, and you'll know immediately that you couldn't be anywhere else in the world. What is it that makes it so unique? Well, its watery cityscape means that much of the centre is off-limits to traffic; its architecture is for the most part on a human rather than a grandiose scale; and its people are comfortable in their skin, proud of the capacity of their city to change, but also of its uncanny – and reassuring – ability to stay much the same as it has always been.

TAKE A BOAT TRIP DOWN THE CANALS

Pocket Rough Guide

AMSTERDAM

written and researched by

MARTIN DUNFORD AND PHIL LEE

In part it's the longstanding liberal tradition of the city that has given Amsterdam its distinctive character, beginning with the obvious – the legalized prostitution and dope-smoking coffeeshops – through to more subtle qualities, encapsulated by Amsterdammers themselves in the word *gezellig*, a very Dutch concept which roughly corresponds to "warmly convivial" – something perhaps most manifest in the city's wonderfully diverse selection of bars and cafés. The city is also riding something of a resurgent wave, with dozens of great new restaurants, a vibrant arts scene and a club scene that has come of age,

not to mention the radical redevelopment of its old docklands and the rediscovery of neighbourhoods like the Oud West, de Pijp and Amsterdam Noord – a process that will only be hastened when they finally complete the Noord-Zuid metro line, whose workings have scarred the city centre for years now.

The old centre of the city spreads south from the train station, and includes Amsterdam's famous Red Light District. The layout of the rest of the city centre is determined by a web of canals radiating out from here to loop right round the centre as the so-called Grachtengordel, a planned, seventeenth-century

Best places for...a cold beer in summer

It's hard to imagine a more chilled-out place than Amsterdam in summer, and a better place to just kick back and drink beer. Here are some of our favourite spots to enjoy an alfresco *vaasje* (glass of beer): > **Het Molenpad p.69** > **Proust p.79** > **'t Smalle p.79**

AMSTERDAM AT NIGHT

When to visit

Amsterdam has warm, mild summers and moderately cold and wet winters. The climate is certainly not severe enough to make much difference to the city's routines, which makes Amsterdam an ideal all-year destination. That said, high summer – roughly late June to August – sees the city's parks packed to the gunnels and parts of the centre almost overwhelmed by tourists. Spring and autumn are not too crowded and can be especially beautiful, with mist hanging over the canals and low sunlight beaming through the cloud cover. Even in January and February, when things can be at their gloomiest, there are compensations – wet cobbles glistening under the street lights and the canals rippled by falling raindrops. In the summer, from around June to August, mosquitoes can be bothersome.

extension to the medieval town, with its tall gabled houses reflected in black-green waters.

There are plenty of first-rate attractions, most notably the Anne Frank Huis, the Rijksmuseum, with its wonderful collection of Dutch paintings, and the peerless Van Gogh Museum, the world's largest collection of the artist's work. But it's not all about the sights: Amsterdam is a great city just to be in, with no attractions so compelling that they have to interrupt lazy days of just wandering the canals and taking in the city at your own pace. Finally, don't forget that Holland is a small country and that there are plenty of compelling attractions close by, not least the small town of Haarlem, with the great Frans Hals Museum, the Zuider Zee villages to the north, and the stunning Keukenhof Gardens – all very easy to reach by public transport.

AMSTERDAM AT A GLANCE

>> EATING

The **food** in the average Dutch restaurant has improved hugely in recent years, and there are many places serving inventive takes on homegrown cuisine. The city also has a good assortment of ethnic restaurants, especially Indonesian, Chinese and Thai. There are also lots of bars – known as *eetcafés* – that serve adventurous food for a decent price in a relaxed and unpretentious setting. Note that the Dutch eat out relatively early, with most restaurants opening at 5.30pm or 6pm and closing around 10pm.

>> COFFEESHOPS

Amsterdam is well known for its coffeeshops, which dispense bags of **cannabis** or **ready-made joints**. The majority of coffeeshops are situated in the Old Centre, and because they're not allowed to advertise their wares you'll need to look at the menu to see what's on offer. The hash you'll come across is pretty self-explanatory, apart from *Pollem*, which is compressed resin and stronger than normal. Grass is a different story, with limitless varieties of Dutch weed, grown under artificial lights. Most of it is extremely potent and to be handled with care – ask before you buy and avoid any unpleasant surprises. Most coffeeshops open at 10am or 11am and close around midnight.

>> SHOPPING

The **Nieuwendijk/Kalverstraat** strip in the Old Centre is home to high-street fashion and mainstream department stores, while nearby **Koningsplein** and **Leidsestraat** offer designer clothes and shoe stores. You'll find more offbeat clothes shops in the Jordaan and in the small radial streets that connect the main canals – an area known as the Nine Streets. The cream of Amsterdam's antique trade is in the Spiegelkwartier, centred on **Nieuwe Spiegelstraat**. As regards **opening hours**, many shops take Monday morning off; Thursday is late-opening night, with most places staying open until 9pm.

>> DRINKING & NIGHTLIFE

Amsterdam's selection of bars range from traditional **brown cafés** – cosy places so called because of the dingy colour of their walls, stained by years of tobacco smoke – to slick **designer bars**. Most places stay open until around midnight or 1am during the week, and until 2am at weekends. Look out for the few **tasting houses** or *proeflokalen* that are left, originally the sampling rooms of small private distillers, now tiny, stand-up places specializing in *jenever* (gin); they tend to close around 8pm. The **clubbing** scene is intense, and there are lots of bars with DJs, as well as a decent array of live music options, particularly for jazz.

OUR RECOMMENDATIONS ON WHERE TO EAT, DRINK AND SHOP ARE LISTED AT THE END OF EACH PLACES CHAPTER.

Day One in Amsterdam

1 Dam Square > p.36. The heart of the city, and what better place to start?

2 Royal Palace > p.37. The confidence and pride of the Golden Age – in a building.

3 Nieuwe Kerk > p.38. No longer used as a church, but still one of the city's most impressive Gothic buildings.

4 Nine Streets > p.58. These streets connecting the main canals are the epitome of what makes Amsterdam special – full of intriguing one-off shops and cafés.

Lunch at Greenwoods > p.66. Stop off for a club sandwich by the canal at this pocket-sized gem.

5 The Grachtengordel > p.52–71. After shopping, just get lost in the web of stately seventeenth-century canals that make Amsterdam so unique.

6 Westerkerk > p.57. Rembrandt's burial place, and the city's grandest Renaissance-era landmark.

7 Anne Frank Huis > p.56. The city's most renowned – and moving – sight, bar none.

8 The Jordaan > p.72. One of the city's most wanderable and picturesque districts, full of independent stores, bars and restaurants.

Dinner at Toscanini > p.78. There's no better place to wind up of an evening than at this big, lively and very authentic Italian in the Jordaan.

Day Two in Amsterdam

1 Rijksmuseum > p.95. When it finally reopens this should be one of the finest museums in Europe; for the moment it still gives a decent glimpse of the art of the city's Golden Age.

2 Van Gogh Museum > p.97. The greatest collection of the prolific nineteenth-century artist's work by far, and with good temporary exhibits too.

 Lunch at Loetje > p.101. Lunch on the best steaks and burgers in town, on a lovely outside terrace.

3 Begijnhof > p.44. Tucked away just off the city's main shopping street, this is an alluring unusual oasis of peace in the heart of the city.

4 Amsterdams Historisch Museum > p.45. The history of the city, well told with lots of fascinating original artefacts, all housed in a former orphanage.

5 Red Light District > p.39. It's hard to come to Amsterdam and not have a wander around its most notorious neighbourhood.

6 Oude Kerk > p.38. Despite being right at the centre of the Red Light District, this is the city's most interesting and historic church.

7 Amstelkring > p.40. Better-known now, but this clandestine Catholic church is still something of a hidden gem.

 Dinner at Blauw aan de Waal > p.49. Enjoy a refined dinner in relaxed surroundings, yet still in the heart of the Red Light District.

Jewish Amsterdam

Amsterdam's Jewish Quarter is a shadow of its former self, but there are many reminders of how integral to the life of the city its Jewish population once was. Touring these sights makes for a cohesive and moving day out, especially if you wind up at the most famous Jewish sight of them all, the Anne Frank Huis.

1 Jodenbreestraat > p.82.
The heart of Amsterdam's mainly Sephardic Jewish community in seventeenth-century Amsterdam.

2 Waterlooplein > p.83. Home of the first Jewish settlement in Amsterdam, now the venue of the best flea market.

3 Joods Historisch Museum > p.85. Four converted synagogues house permanent and temporary exhibits on Jewish life in the city.

4 Esnoga > p.84. The city's Portuguese Synagogue was once one of the largest in the world.

5 Hollandse Schouwburg > p.87. The remains of a theatre that was the main assembly point for Jews being deported in World War II.

6 Verzetsmuseum > p.88. Excellent museum dedicated to the wartime resistance to the Nazis.

🍴 **Lunch at Greetje** > p.92. Try out some Dutch cuisine at the snug *Greetje*.

7 Gassan Diamonds > p.81. The only remnant of the main industry of the Jewish Quarter before the war.

8 Anne Frank Huis > p.56. Not in the Jewish Quarter proper, but still the city's principal – and only essential – Jewish sight.

🍴 **Dinner at De Reiger** > p.77. Enjoy a casual dinner at one of the Jordaan's best brown cafés.

Free Amsterdam

You could have a great day out in Amsterdam, see loads, and not spend a cent apart from a few euros on lunch and dinner. Here's how.

1 Schuttersgalerij > p.45. This gallery, with its portraits of civic guards, is the only free bit of the Amsterdam Historical Museum.

2 Begijnhof > p.44. One of the city centre's most beguiling sights, and totally free.

3 Bloemenmarkt > p.63. There's no charge to wander past the stalls of the city's wonderful flower market.

🍴 **Lunch: Cone of chips from Vlaminckx** >p.48. A cone of *frites* from this famed takeaway will only set you back a couple of euros.

4 Albert Cuypmarkt > p.103. Just wandering the length of the city's best market is a fine way to pass the time.

5 Lunchtime concerts at the Concertgebouw/Muziektheater > p.98/p.82. There are regular free lunchtime concerts at these two venues.

6 Vondelpark > p.98. The city centre's main park is one its best attractions, and there's no charge for its weekend summer concerts either.

7 Openbare Bibliotheek > The city's new library just east of Centraal Station on Oosterdokskade is a great building, and a fantastic place to browse books and magazines, and the internet. [MAP - p.82]

8 Ferries across the IJ > Take one of the free ferries to suburban Amsterdam from the rear of Centraal Station.

🍴 **Dinner: Keuken van 1870** > p.49. An authentically Dutch dinner at this long-established and excellent cheapie.

Big sights

1 **Van Gogh Museum** With the world's most comprehensive collection of the artist's work, this museum is simply unmissable. **>** **p.97**

2 Red Light District Although recently spruced up, Amsterdam's red light district is still the real thing – and a big attraction in its own right. > **p.39**

3 Vondelpark The leafy Vondelpark, with its ponds, footpaths and parrots, is the city centre's most attractive park. > **p.98**

4 Anne Frank Huis The secret annexe where the diarist hid with her family during the Nazi occupation is Amsterdam's most moving tourist attraction. > **p.56**

5 Royal Palace The supreme architectural example of the Dutch empire at the height of its powers. > **p.37**

Museums and galleries

1 Rijksmuseum Only partly open for the moment, but it's the place to see the best of the city's collection of seventeenth-century Dutch art. **> p.95**

2 Amstelkring Once a clandestine church for the city's Catholics, the seventeenth-century house chapel is a very distinctive sight. > **p.40**

4 Verzetsmuseum This museum brilliantly charts the history of the Dutch resistance to the Nazis through a mixture of exhibits. > **p.88**

3 Van Gogh Museum The greatest collection of Van Gogh's work, along with the paintings and Japanese prints that influenced him. > **p.97**

5 Amsterdams Historisch Museum An excellent museum devoted to the life and times of the city. > **p.45**

Waterfront

1 **Queen's Day** The one day of the year when anarchy reigns on the city's canals. Don't miss it. > **p.136**

2 **Brouwersgracht** The dolled-up former warehouses here make this one of the city's most picturesque canals. **> p.52**

3 **Blijburg** The ultimate urban beach in summer. **> p.91**

4 **The Sluyswacht** This bar in a rickety old lock-keeper's house is a wonderful place to have a drink. **> p.93**

5 **Zeeburg** Cutting-edge new architecture and design, and lots of waterside bars and restaurants to enjoy it from. **> p.90**

Coffeeshops

1 Abraxas Lots of levels to negotiate via spiral staircases make this cosy place challenging after a spliff or two. **>** **p.47**

2 Kadinsky Always busy, and serves great cookies and hot chocolate too. > **p.47**

3 Hill Street Blues
Favoured for its comfy sofas and chilled-out vibe, with two locations right in the heart of the Red Light District. > **p.47**

4 Barney's Coffeeshop Once known for its great breakfast, now for the quality of its dope. > **p.76**

5 Dampkring Loud and friendly city-centre hangout with excellent hash and weed at good prices. > **p.47**

Restaurants

1 Moeders Proper Dutch food at moderate prices. > **p.78**

2 Greetje Great service, fantastic modern Dutch food. > **p.92**

4 Toscanini One of the city centre's best Italian restaurants – big, bustling and authentic. > **p.78**

3 Blauw aan de Wal A wonderful, peaceful culinary haven right in the heart of the Red Light District. > **p.49**

5 De Belhamel Great-value Dutch cooking on picturesque Brouwersgracht. > **p.66**

Bars

1 Wynand Fockink Perhaps the city's best example of an old-fashioned *proeflokaal* or "tasting-house". **> p.51**

2 In 't Aepjen Right on Zeedijk, this is one of the city's top brown cafés. **> p.51**

3 Café 't Arendsnest This friendly canal house bar is the best place to try Dutch beers from all over the country. **> p.68**

5 't Smalle One of the city's oldest and cosiest cafés, with a lovely waterside terrace. **> p.79**

4 Hoppe There's nowhere quite like *Hoppe*, or the crowd that winds up here, especially after everywhere else has closed. **> p.51**

Nightlife and Culture

1 Bimhuis Amsterdam's premier jazz venue, next door to the Muziekgebouw.
> **p.93**

2 Jimmy Woo East meets West at this loungey club, where the stylish come out to play and the dancefloor heaves to the sound of disco and club classics. > **p.71**

4 Melkweg This Sixties favourite remains the city's prime venue for inventive and original performing arts. > **p.71**

3 Bitterzoet Spacious but snug bar and theatre that hosts club nights and early evening live music and performance art. > **p.51**

5 Paradiso One of the city's oldest venue for live music, and still the best. > **p.27**

Shopping

1 Puccini The chocolates are made on the premises and are unusually good at their two city centre locations. > **p.47 & 65**

2 The Nine Streets Hosts some of the city's quirkiest one-off stores – well worth a wander. **> p.58**

3 Condomerie Het Gulden Vlies The ultimate specialist shop, and a useful one too, with a mind-boggling array of prophylactics. **> p.46**

5 Droog Not quite like any other shop you may have been to... **> p.46**

4 Albert Cuypmarkt Busy general market that is still to some extent the authentic heart of working-class Amsterdam. **> p.103**

PLACES

The Old Centre

Amsterdam's most vivacious district, the Old Centre is a tangle of antique streets and narrow canals, confined in the north by the River IJ and to the west and south by the Singel. Given the dominance of Centraal Station on most transport routes, this is where you'll almost certainly arrive. From here a stroll across the bridge will take you onto the Damrak, which divided the Oude Zijde (Old Side) of the medieval city to the east from the smaller Nieuwe Zijde (New Side) to the west. It also leads to the heart of the Old Centre, Dam Square, the site of the city's most imperious building, the Royal Palace (Koninklijk Paleis). Nowadays much of the Oude Zijde is taken up by the city's notorious Red Light District – but the area is about more than just sleaze: its main canals and the houses that line them are among Amsterdam's most handsome. And the Old Centre as a whole hosts some of the city's best bars and restaurants alongside the tourist tat.

CENTRAAL STATION

MAP PP.34–35, POCKET MAP C10–C11

With its high gables and cheerful brickwork, **Centraal Station** is an imposing prelude to the city. Built in the 1880s, it aroused much controversy because it effectively separated the centre from the River IJ, source of the city's wealth, for the first time in Amsterdam's long history. Inside, the cavernous main booking hall and grand arches have a suitable sense of occasion, and from here the whole of Amsterdam lies before you. However, for the moment, **Stationsplein** just outside is a pretty unprepossessing introduction to the city: a messy open space, edged by ovals of water and cut through by trams. It's currently dominated by the building works of the city's new north-south transport link, which are taking a lot longer than expected. Once they're complete, expect a much spruced-up open space (see box opposite).

TRAMS AT CENTRAAL STATION

ST NICOLAASKERK

Prins Hendrikkade. Mon & Sat noon–3pm,
Tues–Fri 11am–4pm. Free. MAP PP.34–35, POCKET
MAP D11

Dating back to the 1880s, the
city's foremost Catholic
church, with its whopping
twin towers and spacious
interior is dedicated to the
patron saint of sailors – and
of Amsterdam. Above the
altar is the crown of the
Habsburg Emperor
Maximilian, very much a
symbol of the city.

DAMRAK

MAP PP.34–35, POCKET MAP C11

Running from Centraal Station
to Dam Square, **Damrak** was a
canal and the city's main
nautical artery until 1672, when
it was filled in – much to the
relief of the locals, who were
tired of the stink. With the
docks moved elsewhere,
Damrak became a busy
commercial drag, as it remains
today: an unenticing avenue
lined with tacky restaurants,
bars and bureaux de change.

Got the builders in?

The station area and inner harbour have frankly looked a bit of a mess for
as long as most people can remember, due to a long-running project to
redevelop the station and the surrounding area at the same time while
building a new metro line to link the city centre with the south of the city and
the resurgent north across the IJ. City centre stations are to be built at
Centraal Station, Rokin and the Vijzelgracht, and for the best part of six years
now the area around Stationsplein has been a massive construction site
– and the chaos looks set to continue for some time, at least until the
completion of the project in 2015. There has been huge controversy over the
plan: some question whether it's even possible to build a tunnel under a city
centre that is mainly built on wooden stilts, and work was halted for a while a
couple of years back when a number of buildings began to collapse. But the
authorities are determined to press on, and claim they will not only deliver
better connections between the city centre and outlying districts, but also a
pedestrian-friendly Stationsplein and inner harbour. Whatever the result, it
will seem like an improvement after the last couple of years.

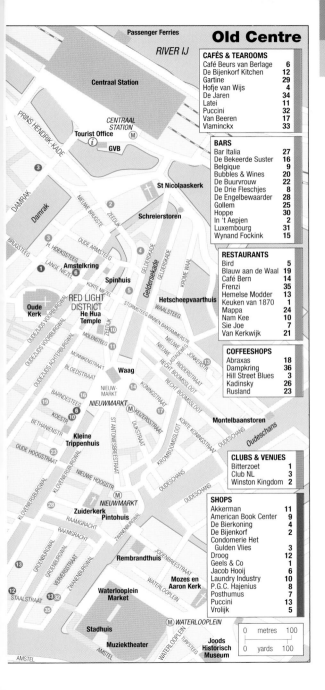

Old Centre

Passenger Ferries

RIVER IJ

Centraal Station

CENTRAAL STATION

PRINS HENDRIK-KADE

Tourist Office (ℹ) (M)

GVB

DAMRAK

Damrak

BRUGSTEEG

St Nicolaaskerk

NIEUWE BRUGSTEEG

ZEEDIJK

Schreierstoren

OUDE ARMSTEEG

H. HOEKSSTEEG

LANGE NIEZEL

Amstelkring

Spinhuis

KORTE NIEZEL

GELDERSKADE

GELDERSKADE

KROME WAAL

Oude Kerk

RED LIGHT DISTRICT

He Hua Temple

OUDEZIJDS VOORBURGWAL

OUDEZIJDS VOORBURGWAL

OUDEZIJDS ACHTERBURGWAL

STORMSTEEG BINNEN BANTAMMERSTR

Hetscheepvaarthuis

WAALSTEEG

ZEEDIJK

MOLENSTEEG

MONNIKENSTRAAT

BLOEDSTRAAT

NIEUWE HOOGSTR

NIEUWE JONKERSTR

RECHT BOOMSSLOOT

RECHT BOOMSSLOOT

Waag

BARNDESTEEG

NIEUW-MARKT

KONINGSTRAAT

KEIZERSSTRAAT

KOESTR

NIEUWMARKT (M)

KORTE KONINGSTRAAT

ST ANTONIESBREESTRAAT

DIJKSTRAAT

KROMBOOMSSLOOT

OUDESCHANS

Montelbaanstoren

Oudeschans

BETHANIENSTR

Kleine Trippenhuis

OUDE HOOGSTRAAT

KLOVENIERSBURGWAL

NIEUWE HOOGSTR

KLOVENIERSBURGWAL

NIEUWMARKT (M)

Zuiderkerk

Pintohuis

RAAMGRACHT

ZWANENBURGWAL

JODENBREESTRAAT

GROENBURGWAL

GROENBURGWAL

Rembrandthuis

VERWERSTRAAT

ZWANENBURGWAL

Mozes en Aaron Kerk

STAALSTRAAT

Waterlooplein Market

WATERLOOPLEIN

WATERLOOPLEIN

Stadhuis

Muziektheater

AMSTEL

AMSTEL

(M) WATERLOOPLEIN

WATERLOOPLEIN

TURFSTEEG

Joods Historisch Museum

CAFÉS & TEAROOMS

Café Beurs van Berlage	6
De Bijenkorf Kitchen	12
Gartine	29
Hofje van Wijs	4
De Jaren	34
Latei	11
Puccini	32
Van Beeren	17
Vlaminckx	33

BARS

Bar Italia	27
De Bekeerde Suster	16
Belgique	9
Bubbles & Wines	20
De Buurvrouw	22
De Drie Fleschjes	8
De Engelbewaarder	28
Gollem	25
Hoppe	30
In 't Aepjen	2
Luxembourg	31
Wynand Fockink	15

RESTAURANTS

Bird	5
Blauw aan de Waal	19
Café Bern	14
Frenzi	35
Hemelse Modder	13
Keuken van 1870	1
Mappa	24
Nam Kee	10
Sie Joe	7
Van Kerkwijk	21

COFFEESHOPS

Abraxas	18
Dampkring	36
Hill Street Blues	7
Kadinsky	26
Rusland	23

CLUBS & VENUES

Bitterzoet	1
Club NL	3
Winston Kingdom	2

SHOPS

Akkerman	11
American Book Center	9
De Bierkoning	4
De Bijenkorf	2
Condomerie Het Gulden Vlies	3
Droog	12
Geels & Co	1
Jacob Hooij	6
Laundry Industry	10
P.G.C. Hajenius	8
Posthumus	7
Puccini	13
Vrolijk	5

0	metres	100
0	yards	100

THE BEURS VAN BERLAGE

Damrak 277 Ⓦ www.beursvanberlage.nl.
MAP PP.34–35, POCKET MAP B11–C11

The imposing bulk of the **Beurs** – the old Stock Exchange – is a seminal work designed at the turn of the twentieth century by the leading light of the Dutch modern movement, **Hendrik Petrus Berlage**. Berlage re-routed Dutch architecture with this building, forsaking the classicism that had dominated the nineteenth century for a modern style with cleaner lines. The Beurs has long since lost its commercial function and today it's used for exhibitions, concerts and conferences, which means that sometimes you can go in, sometimes you can't. Inside, the main hall is distinguished by the graceful lines of its exposed ironwork and its shallow-arched arcades as well as the fanciful frieze celebrating the stockbroker's trade. If it's closed, stop by the café that fronts onto Beursplein around the corner (see p.48) for a coffee and admire the tiled scenes of the past, present and the future by Jan Toorop.

DAM SQUARE

MAP PP.34–35, POCKET MAP B12

It was **Dam Square** that gave Amsterdam its name: in the thirteenth century the River Amstel was dammed here, and the fishing village that grew around it became known as "Amstelredam". Boats could sail into the square down the Damrak and unload right in the middle of the settlement, which soon prospered by trading herrings for Baltic grain. Today it's an open and airy but somehow rather desultory square, despite the presence of the main municipal war memorial, a prominent stone tusk adorned by bleak, suffering figures and decorated with the coats of arms of each of the Netherlands' provinces (plus the ex-colony of Indonesia). The Amsterdam branch of **Madame Tussaud's** waxworks is here, at no. 20 (daily: Jan–March & Nov–Dec 10am–5.30pm; April–June & Sept–Oct 10am–6.30pm; July 10am–8.30pm; Aug 10am–9.30pm; last entry 1hr before closing; €21, children 5–15 €16; Ⓦwww .madametussauds.nl).

THE ROYAL PALACE

Dam ☎ 020/620 4060, 🌐 www.paleisamsterdam
.nl. Tues–Sun noon–5pm, July & Aug 11am–
5pm. €7.50. MAP PP.34–35, POCKET MAP B12

Dominating Dam Square is the
Royal Palace – Koninklijk
Paleis – though the title is
deceptive, given that this vast
structure started out as the city's
town hall and only had its first
royal occupant when Louis
Bonaparte, brother of
Napoleon, moved in during the
French occupation.

At the time of the building's
construction in the
mid-seventeenth century,
Amsterdam was at the height of
its powers, and the city council
craved a residence that was a
suitable declaration of its wealth
and independence. They opted
for a progressive design by
Jacob van Campen, and in 1648
work started on what was then
the largest town hall in Europe.
The exterior is full of
symbolism, with a couple of
depictions of Amsterdam as a
port and trading centre – the
tableau at the front is presided
over by Neptune and a veritable
herd of unicorns. The interior,
too, proclaims the pride and
confidence of the time, in
particular the lavish Citizen's
Hall, a handsome marble
chamber situated at the heart of
the building. Here the
enthroned figure of Amsterdam
sits over the entrance, flanked
by figures representing Strength
and Wisdom; at the opposite
end, the figure of Justice
perches over the entrance to the
Magistrates' Chamber, below
another giant figure of Atlas.

Start your tour here and
follow the rooms around,
taking in the witty symbolism
that pervades the building:
cocks fight above the entrance
to the Commissioner of Petty
Affairs, while Apollo, god of the
sun and the arts, brings
harmony to the disputes;
outside the Bankruptcy
Chamber a relief shows the Fall
of Icarus, above which marble
carvings depicting hungry rats
scurrying around an empty
chest and unpaid bills; and two
large paintings in the
Burgomasters' Cabinet, one by
Ferdinand Bol the other by
Govert Flinck, show how the
burgomasters fancied
themselves above corruption in
the manner of Roman Consuls.
The Burgomasters' Chamber,
next door, looks down on the
ground-floor Tribunal, where
they gave advice to the judges
sitting on the marble benches as
they passed judgement on
hapless criminals.

THE ROYAL PALACE

1

1

0

1

1

OUDE KERK

THE NIEUWE KERK

Dam ☏ 020/638 6909, ⓦ www.nieuwekerk.nl.
Daily 10am–5pm, Thurs until 10pm. €8
MAP PP.34-35, POCKET MAP B12

Vying for importance with the Royal Palace is the adjacent **Nieuwe Kerk**, which despite its name – "new church" – is an early fifteenth-century structure built in a late flourish of the Gothic style, with a forest of pinnacles and high, slender gables. Nowadays it's de-sanctified and used for temporary exhibitions. Opening times vary according to what's on, and occasionally it's closed altogether when changing exhibitions. But it is worth going in if you can: its hangar-like interior holds a scattering of decorative highlights, such as the seventeenth-century tomb of Dutch naval hero Admiral Michiel de Ruyter, complete with trumpeting angels, conch-blowing Neptunes and cherubs all in a tizzy.

MAGNA PLAZA

Nieuwezijds Voorburgwal ⓦ www.magnaplaza .nl. Mon 11am–7pm, Tues–Sat 10am–7pm, Thurs until 9pm, Sun noon–7pm. MAP PP.34-35, POCKET MAP A12

Behind the Royal Palace, you can't miss the old neo-Gothic post office of 1899, now converted into the **Magna Plaza** shopping mall, housing numerous clothes chains.

OUDE KERK

Oudekerksplein ⓦ www.oudekerk.nl.
Mon–Sat 11am–5pm, Sun 1–5pm. €5.
MAP PP.34-35, POCKET MAP C12

The **Oude Kerk** is the city's most appealing church. There's been a church on this site since the middle of the thirteenth century, but most of the present building dates from a century later, funded by the pilgrims who came here in their hundreds following a widely publicized miracle. The story goes that in 1345 a dying man regurgitated the Host he had received here at Communion and when it was thrown on the fire afterwards, it did not burn. The unburnable Host was placed in a chest and eventually installed here, and although it disappeared during the Reformation, thousands of the faithful still come to take part in the annual commemorative **Stille Omgang** in mid-March, a silent nocturnal procession terminating at the Oude Kerk. Inside you can see the unadorned memorial tablet of Rembrandt's first wife, Saskia van Uylenburg, beneath the smaller of the organs, and three beautifully coloured stained-glass windows beside the ambulatory dating from the 1550s. Oude Kerk's tower is open weekends (April–Sept 1–4.30pm; €6).

The Red Light District

The area immediately to the east of Damrak is the **Red Light District**, known locally as "De Walletjes" (Small Walls) on account of the series of low brick walls that contains its canals. The district stretches across the two narrow canals that once marked the eastern part of medieval Amsterdam – Oudezijds Voorburgwal and Oudezijds Achterburgwal – with the far canal of Kloveniersburgwal forming its eastern boundary. Despite auspicious beginnings as the aptly named "Velvet Canal" – look out for the handsome facades of Oudezijds Voorburgwal that recall ritzier days – nowadays the area is full of the "window brothels", sex shops and porn cinemas and theatres that have long been one of the city's most distinctive draws, the girls in particular drawing crowd of goggling tourists and potential customers in equal measure.

There's an undertow to the district, however, that isn't particularly pleasant. Many of the girls are illegal immigrants, who hand over a fair percentage of their earnings to their pimps, and the city has taken action over recent years to crack down on the number of women working here, buying up some of the buildings and encouraging other sorts of business to flourish – you'll notice the odd window with a design or fashion display. But there's no doubt that for the moment at least, sex is still the main event here. The **Prostitution Information Centre**, at Enge Kerksteeg 3, runs Red Light District tours (Sat 5pm; €12.50) if you want to know more, while on a more frivolous note you may want to check out the **Erotic Museum**, Oudezijds Achterburgwal 54 (daily 11am–1am; €7), or the slightly better value **Sex Museum**, five minutes' walk away at Damrak 18 (daily 9.30am–11.30pm; €4) – both of which have several floors of porn and erotica through the ages to entertain you. One word of warning: don't even think about taking a picture of one of the windows, unless you're prepared for some major grief from the camera-shy prostitutes or their minders.

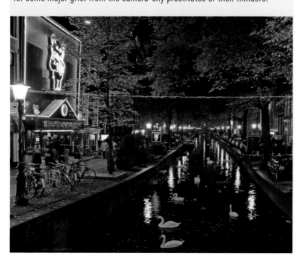

THE AMSTELKRING

Oudezijds Voorburgwal 40 ⓦ www
.museumamstelkring.nl. Mon–Sat 10am–5pm,
Sun 1–5pm. €7. MAP PP.34–35, POCKET MAP C11

A few metres north of the
Oude Kerk is the lovely
Amstelkring, a former
Catholic church, now one of
Amsterdam's most enjoyable
museums. The Amstelkring –
"Amstel Circle" – is named
after the group of nineteenth-
century historians who saved
the building from demolition,
but its proper name is Ons
Lieve Heer Op Solder ("Our
Dear Lord in the Attic"). The
church dates from the early
seventeenth century when,
with the Protestants firmly in
control, the city's Catholics
were only allowed to practise
their faith in private – as here
in this clandestine church,
which occupies the loft of a
wealthy merchant's house. The
church's narrow nave has been
skilfully shoehorned into the
available space and, flanked by
elegant balconies, there's just
enough room for an ornately

carved organ at one end and a
mock-marble high altar,
decorated with Jacob de Wit's
mawkish *Baptism of Christ*, at
the other. The rest of the house
is similarly untouched, its
original furnishings
reminiscent of interiors by
Vermeer or De Hooch.

HASH MARIHUANA HEMP MUSEUM

Oudezijds Achterburgwal 148 & 130 ⓣ 020/623
5961. ⓦ www.hashmuseum.com. Daily
10am–11pm. €9. MAP PP.34–35, POCKET MAP C12

The **Hash Marihuana Hemp
Museum** features displays on
different kinds of dope and the
huge number of ways to
imbibe and otherwise use it,
both here and in the associated
Hemp Gallery a few doors
down. There's also an indoor
marijuana garden, samples of
textiles and paper made with
hemp, and pamphlets
explaining the medicinal
properties of cannabis, and, of
course, a shop selling pipes,
books, videos and plenty of
souvenirs.

NIEUWMARKT

MAP PP.34–35, POCKET MAP C12

On the far side of the Red Light
District is the Nieuwmarkt, a
wide open cobbled square that
was long one of the city's most
important markets. Its main
focus is the multi-turreted
Waag, a delightful building
dating from the 1480s, when it
served as one of the city's
fortified gates, the Sint
Antoniespoort, before being
turned into a municipal
weighing-house (*waag*), with
the rooms upstairs taken over
by the surgeons' guild. It was
here that the surgeons held
lectures on anatomy and public
dissections, the inspiration for
Rembrandt's famous *Anatomy
Lesson of Dr Tulp*. It has now

THE AMSTELKRING

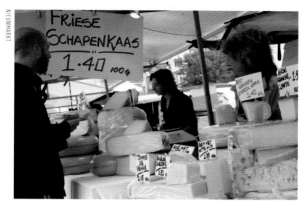

been converted into a café-bar and restaurant, *In de Waag*.

THE SCHREIERSTOREN

Geldersekade. MAP PP.34–35, POCKET MAP D11–D12

A few minutes' walk north from Nieuwmarkt, the squat **Schreierstoren** (Weepers' Tower) is a rare surviving chunk of the city's medieval wall. Originally, the tower overlooked the River IJ and it was here (legend has it) that women gathered to watch their menfolk sail away – hence its name. A badly weathered stone plaque inserted in the wall is a reminder of all those sad goodbyes, and another much more recent plaque recalls the departure of Henry Hudson from here in 1609, when he stumbled across an island the locals called Manhattan.

HET SCHEEPVAARTHUIS

Prins Hendrikkade 108. MAP PP.34–35, POCKET MAP D12

Now occupied by the five-star *Amrath* hotel, this is one of the city's most flamboyant Art Deco buildings, covered with a welter of marine connections – the entrance is shaped like the prow of a ship, and surmounted by statues of Poseidon and his wife, and representations of the four points of the compass.

KLOVENIERSBURGWAL

MAP PP.34–35, POCKET MAP C12–C13

Nieuwmarkt lies at the northern end of Kloveniersburgwal, a long, dead-straight waterway framed by old, dignified facades. One house of special note is the **Trippenhuis**, at no. 29, a huge overblown mansion complete with Corinthian pilasters and a grand frieze built for the Trip family in 1662. One of the richest families in Amsterdam, the Trips were one of a clique of families (Six, Trip, Hooft and Pauw) who shared power during the city's Golden Age.

Almost directly opposite, on the west bank of the canal, the **Kleine Trippenhuis** at no. 26 is, by contrast, one of the narrowest houses in Amsterdam, complete with a warmly carved facade with a balustrade featuring centaurs and sphinxes. Legend asserts that Mr Trip's coachman was so taken aback by the size of the new family mansion that he exclaimed he would be happy with a home no wider than the Trips' front door – which is exactly what he got.

ST ANTONIESBREESTRAAT

MAP PP.34–35, POCKET MAP C12–C13

Stretching south from the wide open spaces of the Nieuwmarkt, **St Antoniesbreestraat** once linked the city centre with the Jewish quarter, but its huddle of shops and houses was mostly demolished in the 1980s to make way for a main road. The plan was subsequently abandoned, but the modern buildings that now line most of the street hardly fire the soul, even if the modern symmetries – and cubist, coloured panels – of the apartment blocks that spill along part of the street are visually arresting.

THE PINTOHUIS

St Antoniesbreestraat 69. Mon & Wed 2–8pm, Fri 2–5pm, Sat 11am–4pm. Free. MAP PP.34–35, POCKET MAP D13

One of the few survivors of all this development is the **Pintohuis**, which is now a public library. Easily spotted by its off-white Italianate facade, the mansion is named after Isaac de Pinto, a Jew who fled Portugal to escape the Inquisition and subsequently became a founder of the East India Company. Pinto bought the property in 1651 and promptly had it remodelled in grand style, the facade interrupted by six lofty pilasters, which lead the eye up to the blind balustrade. The mansion was the talk of the town, even more so when Pinto had the interior painted in a similar style to the front – pop in to look at the birds and cherubs of the original painted ceiling.

THE ZUIDERKERK

Mon–Fri 9am–5pm, Sat noon–4pm. Free. MAP PP.34–35, POCKET MAP C13

The **Zuiderkerk** dates from 1611 and was designed by the prolific architect and sculptor Hendrick de Keyser, whose distinctive – and very popular – style extrapolated elements of traditional Flemish design, with fanciful detail and frilly towers added wherever possible. The soaring tower is typical of his work and comes complete with balconies and balustrades, arches and columns. Now deconsecrated, the church has been turned into a municipal information centre with displays on housing and the environment, plus temporary exhibitions revealing the city council's future plans. The tower, which has a separate entrance, can be climbed during the summer (April–Sept Wed–Sat 2–4pm; €6).

OUDEMANHUISPOORT AND AROUND

MAP PP.34–35, POCKET MAP B14

At the top of Kloveniersburgwal, on the right, the **Oudemanhuispoort** is a covered passageway leading off the street, and is lined with secondhand bookstalls (Mon–

PINTOHUIS

Sat 10am–4pm); it was formerly part of an almshouse complex for elderly men – hence the unusual name. The buildings on either side are part of the University of Amsterdam, which dominates this part of town. You can either wander through its peaceful precincts or, just beyond, cross the south end of **Kloveniersburgwal** to one of the prettiest corners of the city – a small pocket of placid waterways and old canal houses that extends east to **Groenburgwal**, a delightful, dead-end canal.

ROKIN AND KALVERSTRAAT

MAP PP.34–35, POCKET MAP B12–B14

The **Rokin** picks up where the Damrak leaves off, cutting south from Dam Square in a wide sweep that follows the former course of the River Amstel. This was the business centre of the nineteenth-century city, and although it has lost much of its prestige it is still flanked by an attractive medley of architectural styles incorporating everything from grandiose nineteenth-century

mansions to more utilitarian modern stuff. Running parallel, pedestrianized **Kalverstraat** is a busy shopping street that has been a commercial centre since medieval times, when it was used as a calf market; nowadays it's home to many of the city's chain stores and clothes shops – you could be anywhere in Holland really.

ALLARD PIERSON MUSEUM

Oude Turfmarkt 127 ☎ 020/525 2556, ⓦ www.allardpiersonmuseum.nl. Tues–Fri 10am–5pm, Sat & Sun 1–5pm. €6.50. MAP PP.34–35, POCKET MAP B13–B14

A good old-fashioned archeological museum in a solid Neoclassical building dating from the 1860s, the **Allard Pierson Museum** holds a wide-ranging but fairly small collection of finds retrieved from Egypt, Greece and Italy. The particular highlights are the museum's Greek pottery, with fine examples of both the black- and red-figured wares produced in the sixth and fifth centuries BC, and several ornate Roman sarcophagi.

HOTEL DOELEN

Nieuwe Doelenstraat 24. MAP PP.34–35, POCKET MAP C14

Just off Muntplein, the **Hotel Doelen** incorporates the Klovaniers Tower, and was once the headquarters and meeting place of the company Rembrandt depicted in his painting *The Night Watch*. No one knows for sure whether he painted the famous work here, but it certainly hung in the building for a time, and if you ask nicely in reception they will let you stroll up to see where it was, although there's not much to look at beyond crumbling redbrick wall and a bad photo of the painting.

HEILIGEWEG AND SPUI

MAP PP.34-35, POCKET MAP A14

Across Kalverstraat, **Heiligeweg**, or "Holy Way", was once part of a much longer route used by pilgrims heading into Amsterdam. Every other religious reference disappeared centuries ago, but there is one interesting edifice here, the fanciful gateway of the old **Rasphuis** (House of Correction) that now fronts a shopping mall at the foot of Voetboogstraat. The gateway is surmounted by a sculpture of a woman punishing two criminals chained at her sides above the single word "Castigatio" (punishment). Beneath is a carving by Hendrik de Keyser showing wolves and lions cringing before the whip.

Cut up Voetboogstraat and you soon reach the **Spui**, whose west end opens out into a wide, tram-clanking intersection in the middle of which is a cloying statue of a young boy, known as *'t Lieverdje* ("Little Darling" or "Loveable Scamp"), a gift to the city from a cigarette company in 1960. It was here in the mid-1960s, with the statue seen as a symbol of the addicted consumer, that the playful political mavericks, the Provos, organized some of their most successful public pranks. There's a small secondhand book market here on Friday mornings.

THE BEGIJNHOF

ⓦ www.begijnhofamsterdam.nl. Daily 8am–5pm. Free. MAP PP.34-35, POCKET MAP A13

A little gateway on the north side of the Spui leads into the **Begijnhof**, where a huddle of immaculately maintained old houses looks onto a central green; if this door is locked, try the main entrance, just a couple of hundred metres north of the Spui on Gedempte Begijnensloot. The Begijnhof was founded in the fourteenth century as a home for the *beguines* – members of a Catholic sisterhood living as nuns, but without vows and with the right of return to the secular world. The original medieval complex comprised a series of humble brick cottages, but these were mostly replaced by the larger, grander houses of today shortly after the Reformation, though the secretive, enclosed design survived.

The **Engelse Kerk** which takes up one side of the

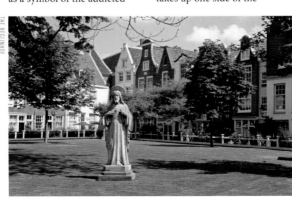

Begijnhof is of medieval construction, but it was taken from the *beguines* and given to Amsterdam's English community during the Reformation and is of interest for the carefully worked panels on the pulpit, which were designed by a youthful Piet Mondriaan. The *beguines*, meanwhile, celebrated Mass inconspicuously in the clandestine Catholic **Begijnhof Kapel**, which they established in the house opposite their old church, and this is still used today, a homely and very devout place, full of paintings and with large balconies on either side of the main nave.

AMSTERDAM'S HISTORISCH MUSEUM

AMSTERDAMS HISTORISCH MUSEUM

Two entrances: Nieuwezijds Voorburgwal 357 & Kalverstraat 92 ☎ 020/523 1822, ⦿ www .ahm.nl. Mon–Fri 10am–5pm, Sat & Sun 11am–5pm. €10. MAP PP.34–35, POCKET MAP A13

Just metres from the Begijnhof, the **Schuttersgalerij** – the Civic Guard Gallery (free) – also accessible from Kalverstraat and St Luciensteeg, is lined by an interesting assortment of group portraits of the Amsterdam militia, painted when the city was at the height of its economic success. The gallery is actually part of the adjoining **Amsterdams Historisch Museum**, which occupies the smartly restored but rambling seventeenth-century buildings of the municipal orphanage. This museum surveys the city's development with a scattering of artefacts and lots of paintings from the thirteenth century onwards – a somewhat garbled collection, but at least the labelling is mostly in English as well as Dutch.

Maps and paintings punctuate the galleries and record the growth of the city, starting with an electronic map showing the city's evolution form the draining of the Amstel in 1274 to the present day. Cornelis Anthonisz's 1538 **Bird's Eye View of Amsterdam** is the oldest surviving plan of the city, and in the next room there are various renderings of the old and new town halls, the latter now the Royal Palace.

High points beyond here include a number of paintings from the city's Golden Age – Rembrandt's wonderful *Anatomy Lesson of Dr Jan Deijman* stands out – and others depicting the regents of several orphanages, smug and content in the company of the grateful poor. But the museum doesn't only focus on the Golden Age, and has objects of interest right up to the modern era, starting with Breitner's depictions of Dam Square from 1898, through the war years and Nazi occupation, to postwar material that includes the CoBrA (see p.107) painter Karel Appel's murals for the town hall (now decorating the city's *Grand Hotel* restaurant) and the liberalization of dope and growth of the city's coffeeshops.

Shops

AKKERMAN

Kalverstraat 149. Mon–Fri 10am–5.45pm, Thurs until 8.45pm, Sat 10am–5pm, Sun 1–5pm. MAP PP.34–35, POCKET MAP B13

The city's poshest pen shop, with an excellent selection of pens and writing accessories.

AMERICAN BOOK CENTER

Spui 12. Mon–Sat 10am–8pm, Thurs until 9pm, Sun 11am–6pm. MAP PP.34–35, POCKET MAP A13

A great stock of books in English, and one of the city's best sources of English-language magazines and newspapers.

DE BIERKONING

Paleisstraat 125. Mon 1–7pm, Tues–Fri 11am–7pm, Sat 11am–6pm, Sun 1–6pm. MAP PP.34–35, POCKET MAP A12

The "Beer King" is aptly named: 950 different beers, with the appropriate glasses to drink them from – just in case you thought beer-drinking could be taken lightly.

DE BIJENKORF

Dam 1. Mon 11am–7pm, Tues, Wed & Sat 9.30am–7pm, Thurs & Fri 10am–9pm, Sun 9.30am–6pm. MAP PP.34–35, POCKET MAP B12

The city's top department store, very slick and good for clothes, accessories and kids' stuff.

CONDOMERIE HET GULDEN VLIES

Warmoesstraat 141. Mon–Sat 11am–6pm. MAP PP.34–35, POCKET MAP B12

Perhaps the world's most famous condom shop, selling condoms of every shape, size and flavour imaginable.

DROOG

Staalstraat 7b. Tues–Sat 11am–6pm, Sun noon–5pm. MAP PP.34–35, POCKET MAP C14

The Amsterdam HQ of the Dutch design collective is a shrine to both simplicity and

AKKERMAN

artsiness, with attention-grabbing furniture, clothes and household objects.

GEELS & CO

Warmoesstraat 67. Mon–Sat 9.30am–6pm. MAP PP.34–35, POCKET MAP C11

Oddly situated among Warmoesstraat's loud bars and porn shops, this is one of the city's oldest and best-equipped coffee and tea specialists, and has a small museum of coffee upstairs.

JACOB HOOIJ

Kloveniersburgwal 10. Mon 1–6pm, Tues–Fri 10am–6pm, Sat 10am–5pm. MAP PP.34–35, POCKET MAP C12

In business at this address since 1778, this is a traditional homeopathic chemist with any amount of herbs and natural cosmetics, as well as a huge stock of *drop* (Dutch liquorice).

LAUNDRY INDUSTRY

Spui 1. Mon–Sat 10am–6pm, Thurs until 9pm, Sun noon–6pm. MAP PP.34–35, POCKET MAP B13

Main Amsterdam branch of this cool Dutch womenswear brand: great clothes, and a nice environment for browsing.

P.G.C. HAJENIUS

Rokin 92. Mon noon–6pm, Tues–Sat 9.30am–6pm, Sun noon–5pm. MAP PP.34–35, POCKET MAP B13

Established tobacconist selling its own and other brands of cigars, tobacco, smoking accessories, and every make of cigarette you can think of.

POSTHUMUS

Sint Luciensteeg 23. Mon noon–5pm, Tues–Fri 9am–5pm, Sat 11am–5pm. MAP PP.34–35, POCKET MAP A13

Posh stationery, cards and, best of all, a choice of hundreds of rubber stamps.

PUCCINI

Staalstraat 17. Mon noon–6pm, Tues–Sat 9am–6pm, Sun noon–5pm. MAP PP.34–35, POCKET MAP C14

Perhaps the best chocolate shop in town – all handmade, with an array of fantastic and imaginative fillings.

VROLIJK

Paleisstraat 135. Mon 11am–6pm, Tues–Fri 10am–6pm, Thurs until 7pm, Sat 10am–5pm, Sun 1–5pm. MAP PP.34–35, POCKET MAP A12

The largest gay and lesbian bookshop in Europe, with books, magazines and videos.

Coffeeshops

ABRAXAS

Jonge Roelensteeg 12. Daily 10am–1am. MAP PP.34–35, POCKET MAP B12

Quirky coffeeshop with spiral staircases that are challenging after a spliff. The hot chocolate with hash is not for the susceptible.

DAMPKRING

Handboogstraat 29. Daily 10am–1am. MAP PP.34–35, POCKET MAP A14

Colourful coffeeshop with a laidback atmosphere that is known for its range of good-quality weed and hash.

HILL STREET BLUES

Warmeosstraat 52a. Daily 9am–1am, Fri & Sat until 3am. MAP PP.34–35, POCKET MAP C11

Cosy, graffitied coffeeshop full of comfy chairs and handily situated next door to a police station – hence the name. Also with a smaller sister branch at Nieuwmarkt 14.

KADINSKY

Rosmarijnsteeg 9. Daily 10am–1am, Fri & Sat until 2am. MAP PP.34–35, POCKET MAP A13

Newly renovated, this is the biggest and best of this small chain of coffeeshops, with good deals and excellent hot chocolate. There's a smaller branch at Langebrugsteeg 9, just off the Rokin.

RUSLAND

Rusland 16. Daily 10am–midnight, Fri & Sat until 1am. MAP PP.34–35, POCKET MAP C13

One of the first Amsterdam coffeeshops, a cramped but vibrant place that's a favourite with both dope fans and tea addicts (it has 40 different kinds).

ABRAXAS

Cafés and tearooms

CAFÉ BEURS VAN BERLAGE

Beursplein 1. Mon–Sat 10am–6pm, Sun 11am–6pm. MAP PP.34–35, POCKET MAP B12

The best chance to glimpse the interior of the Beurs, and an elegantly furnished place to drink coffee or eat lunch.

DE BIJENKORF KITCHEN

Dam 1. Opening times as for the store (see p.46). MAP PP.34–35 , POCKET MAP B12

Great self-service restaurant that's easily the best spot on Damrak to grab a quick spot of lunch – from sandwiches and burgers to sushi and stir-fries – and a nice environment too, with a small terrace that gives good views of the Oude Kerk tower on fine days (see p.46).

GARTINE

Taksteeg 7 Wed–Sun 10am–6pm. MAP PP.34–35, POCKET MAP B13

Tiny place off one of the grungier stretches of Kalverstraat. Nice breakfasts, an array of inventive sandwiches for lunch, and then

– their speciality – high tea served in the afternoon.

HOFJE VAN WIJS

Zeedijk 43. Tues–Fri noon–6pm, Sat & Sun 10am–6pm. MAP PP.34–35, POCKET MAP D11

A hidden treasure in an eighteenth-century courtyard, it sells Indonesian coffee and countless different tea blends.

DE JAREN

Nieuwe Doelenstraat 20. Daily 10am–1am, Fri & Sat until 2am. MAP PP.34–35, POCKET MAP B14

One of the grandest of the grand cafés, overlooking the Amstel next to the university, with three floors and two terraces. A great place to nurse the Sunday papers. It serves reasonably priced food too, and there's a great salad bar.

LATEI

Zeedijk 143. Mon–Wed 8am–6pm, Thurs & Fri 8am–10pm, Sat 9am–10pm, Sun 11am–6pm. MAP PP.34–35, POCKET MAP C12

Homely shop and café that sells bric-a-brac as well as serving good coffee and decent lunches.

PUCCINI

Staalstraat 21. Mon–Fri 8.30am–6pm, Sat & Sun 10am–6pm. MAP PP.34–35, POCKET MAP C14

Lovely café that serves delicious salads, sandwiches and pastries, a few doors down from its sister chocolate shop (see p.47).

VAN BEEREN

Koningstraat 54 Daily 5.30–10.15pm. MAP PP.34–35, POCKET MAP D12

This *eetcafé* serves a satisfying mixture of Dutch staples and modern European fare in relaxed surroundings.

VLAMINCKX

Voetboogstraat 33. Daily noon–6pm. MAP PP.34–35, POCKET MAP A14

Hole-in-the-wall takeaway with a long-established reputation for serving the best *frites* in town.

PUCCINI

Restaurants

BIRD

Zeedijk 77 ☎ 020/420 6289. Daily 2–10pm.
MAP PP.34–35, POCKET MAP D11

This Thai canteen is always packed, and rightly so, for its cheap and authentic Thai fare. Its big brother across the road serves much the same food in slightly more upscale surroundings.

BLAUW AAN DE WAAL

Oudezijds Achterburgwal 99 ☎ 020/330 2257.
Mon–Sat 6–11.30pm. MAP PP.34–35, POCKET MAP C12

Quite a haven, situated down an alley in the heart of the Red Light District, with tremendous French-Dutch food and a wonderfully soothing environment after the mayhem of the streets outside.

CAFÉ BERN

Nieuwmarkt 9 ☎ 020/622 0034. Daily 6–11pm. MAP PP.34–35, POCKET MAP D12

Casual and inexpensive brown café run by a native of Switzerland and patronized by a predominantly arty clientele. Its speciality is, not surprisingly, excellent cheese fondue.

FRENZI

Zwanenburgwal 232 ☎ 020/423.5112. Daily 10am–1am. MAP PP.34–35, POCKET MAP C14

A really busy spot at lunchtime, when it does a stripped-down menu of big sandwiches, salads, soup and a couple of pasta dishes. More upmarket after dark, when its refined and complex regional Italian menu takes over.

HEMELSE MODDER

Oude Waal 9 ☎ 020/624 3203. Daily except Mon 6–11pm. MAP PP.34–35, POCKET MAP D12

Tasty meat, fish and vegetarian food in French-Italian style at reasonable prices in an informal atmosphere. The name "heavenly mud" refers to the dark and white chocolate dessert with vanilla cream.

KEUKEN VAN 1870

Spuistraat 2 ☎ 020/620 4018. Mon–Sat 5–11pm. MAP PP.34–35, POCKET MAP B11

This big, light room has been serving hearty Dutch food to cheapskates for years and continues – justifiably – to thrive. Its three-course €7.50 menu is one of the city's best bargains.

MAPPA

Nes 59 ☎ 020/528 9170. Daily 6–9.45pm, Fri & Sat until10.45pm. MAP PP.34–35, POCKET MAP B13

Classic Italian food with some inventive twists, incorporating good homemade pasta dishes and excellent service in an unpretentious and modern environment.

NAM KEE

Zeedijk 111–113 ☎ 020/624 3470.
MAP PP.34–35, POCKET MAP C12

Arguably the best of a number of cheap Chinese diners along this stretch.

DE JAREN

SIE JOE

Gravenstraat 24 ☎ 020/624 1830. Mon–Sat 11am–7pm, Thurs until 8pm. MAP PP.34–35, POCKET MAP B12

Small Indonesian café-restaurant whose great value-for-money menu is far from extensive but comprises well-prepared, simple dishes such as *gado gado*, *sateh* and *rendang*.

VAN KERKWIJK

Nes 41 ☎ 020/620 3316. Daily 11am–late. MAP PP.34–35, POCKET MAP B12

It looks like a bar but is more of a restaurant these days, serving steaks, fish and so on from an ever-changing menu that isn't written down but is heroically memorized by the attentive waiting staff. Good food, and cheap too – mains from €12.

Bars

BAR ITALIA

Rokin 81/Nes 96. Sun–Thurs 8am–3am, Fri & Sat 8am–4am. MAP PP.34–35, POCKET MAP B13

Very popular and ultra-lively bar of the Italian restaurant downstairs, which goes on noisily into the small hours. The restaurant is open until 11pm.

DE BEKEERDE SUSTER

Kloveniersburgwal 6. Mon–Thurs 3pm–1am, Fri & Sat noon–2am, Sun noon–midnight. MAP PP.34–35, POCKET MAP C12

Don't waste your time in the unappealing drinkeries of the Red Light District proper; this place is a few steps away and offers home-brewed beer, a good bar menu and a very convivial atmosphere, just off the top end of Nieuwmarkt.

BELGIQUE

Gravenstraat 2. Daily 3pm–1am. MAP PP.34–35, POCKET MAP B12

Tiny bar behind the Nieuwe Kerk that serves up Belgian brews along with sounds from a disc-spinning DJ.

BUBBLES & WINES

Nes 37. Mon–Sat 3.30pm–1am, Sun 2–9pm. MAP PP.34–35, POCKET MAP B12

Over 50 wines by the glass in this elegant wine and champagne bar. The knowledgeable staff will help you decide what to have in line with your tastes.

DE BUURVROUW

St Pieterspoortsteeg 29 Mon–Thurs 9pm–3am, Fri–Sun 9pm–4am. MAP PP.34–35, POCKET MAP B13

Dark, noisy late-night bar with pool, DJs and irregular live music.

DE DRIE FLESCHJES

Gravenstraat 18. Mon–Sat noon–8.30pm, Sun 3–8pm. MAP PP.34–35, POCKET MAP B12

Tasting house for spirits and liqueurs. Clients tend to be well heeled or well soused (often both).

DE ENGELBEWAARDER

Kloveniersburgwal 59. Mon–Thurs 11am–1am, Fri & Sat 11am–3am, Sun 2pm–1am. MAP PP.34–35, POCKET MAP C13

Once the meeting place of Amsterdam's bookish types, this is still known as a literary café. It's relaxed and informal, with live jazz on Sunday afternoons.

GOLLEM

Raamsteeg 4. Mon–Fri 4pm–1am, Sat & Sun 2pm–2am. MAP PP.34–35, POCKET MAP A13

Intimate bar with a superb selection of Belgian beers – and with the correct glasses to drink them from. The genial barman will help you choose.

HOPPE

Spui 18. Daily 8am–1am, Fri & Sat until 2am. MAP P.34–35, POCKET MAP A13

One of Amsterdam's oldest and best-known bars, frequented by the city's businessfolk on their way home. Summer is especially good, when the throngs spill out onto the street.

IN 'T AEPJEN

Zeedijk 1. Daily 3pm–1am. MAP PP.34–35, POCKET MAP C11

A bar since the days when Zeedijk was the haunt of sailors on the razzle, and still one of the city centre's best watering holes. Get a plate of cheese or sausage to help the ale go down.

LUXEMBOURG

Spui 22. Daily 9am–1am, Fri & Sat until 2am. MAP PP.34–35, POCKET MAP A13

Crowded, trendy grand café with a long and deep bar, a good selection of snacks, and possibly the best hamburgers in town.

WYNAND FOCKINK

Pijlsteeg 31. Daily 3–9pm. MAP PP.34–35, POCKET MAP B12

Cosy bar hidden just behind the *Krasnapolsky* hotel off Dam

LUXEMBOURG

Square. It offers a vast range of its own flavoured *jenevers* that used to be distilled down the street.

Clubs and venues

BITTERZOET

Spuistraat 2 ☎ 020/521 3001, ⓦ www .bitterzoet.com. Daily 8pm–3am, Fri & Sat & until 4am. MAP PP.34–35, POCKET MAP B11

Bar-cum-club with DJs every night and regular live music too.

CLUB NL

Nieuwezijds Voorburgwal 169 ☎ 020/622 7510, ⓦ www.clubnl.nl. Daily 10pm–3am, Fri & Sat & until 4am. MAP PP.34–35, POCKET MAP A12

What used to be the capital's first lounge bar turned into a posh and stylish house club, frequented by the rich and famous.

WINSTON KINGDOM

Warmoesstraat 131 ☎ 020/623 1380, ⓦ www .winston.nl. Daily 9pm–3am, Fri & Sat until 4am. Tickets €5–9. MAP PP.34–35, POCKET MAP C12

Underground venue in the heart of the red light district, hosting everything from DJ nights to band competitions, movie screenings and themed parties.

The Grachtengordel

The Grachtengordel, or "girdle of canals", reaches right round the city centre and is without doubt the most charming part of Amsterdam, its lattice of olive-green waterways and dinky humpback bridges overlooked by street upon street of handsome seventeenth-century canal houses. It's a subtle cityscape – full of surprises, with a bizarre carving here, an unusual facade there, but it is the district's overall atmosphere that appeals rather than any specific sight, with the exception of the Anne Frank Huis. There's no obvious walking route around the Grachtengordel, and you may prefer to wander around as the mood takes you, but the description we've given below goes from north to south, taking in all the highlights on the way. On all three of the main canals – Herengracht, Keizersgracht and Prinsengracht – street numbers begin in the north and increase as you go south.

BROUWERSGRACHT

MAP PP.54–55, POCKET MAP C1–D2

Running east to west along the northern edge of the three main canals is leafy, memorably picturesque **Brouwersgracht**. Originally, Brouwersgracht lay at the edge of Amsterdam's great harbour with easy access to the sea. This was where ships returning from the East unloaded their silks and spices and breweries flourished here too, capitalizing on their ready access to shipments of fresh water. Today, the harbour bustle has moved elsewhere, and the warehouses, with their distinctive spout-neck gables and shuttered windows, formerly used for the delivery and dispatch of goods by pulley from the canal below, have been converted into ritzy apartments that have proved particularly attractive to actors and film producers. There are handsome merchants' houses here as well, plus moored houseboats and a string of quaint little swing bridges. Restaurants have sprung up here too, including one of the city's best, *De Belhamel* (see p.66).

BROUWERSGRACHT

The canals

The canals of the Grachtengordel were dug in the seventeenth century in order to extend the boundaries of a city no longer able to accommodate its burgeoning population. Increasing the area of the city from two to seven square kilometres was a monumental task, and the conditions imposed by the council were strict. The three main waterways – Herengracht, Keizersgracht and Prinsengracht – were set aside for the residences and businesses of the richer and more influential Amsterdam merchants, while the radial cross-streets were reserved for more modest artisans' homes; meanwhile, immigrants, newly arrived to cash in on Amsterdam's booming economy, were assigned, albeit informally, the Jodenhoek (see p.80) and the Jordaan (see p.72). In the Grachtengordel, everyone, even the wealthiest merchant, had to comply with a set of detailed planning regulations. In particular, the council prescribed the size of each building plot – the frontage was set at thirty feet, the depth two hundred – and although there was a degree of tinkering, the end result was the loose conformity you can see today: tall, narrow residences, whose individualism is mainly restricted to the stylistic permutations amongst the **gables**.

The earliest gables,dating from the early seventeenth century, are the so-called **crow-stepped** gables, which were largely superseded by **neck gables** and **bell gables**, both named for the shape of the gable top. Some are embellished, some aren't, many have decorative cornices and the fanciest – which mostly date from the eighteenth century – sport full-scale balustrades. The plainest gables belong to the warehouses, where deep-arched and shuttered windows line up on either side of the loft doors that were once used for loading and unloading goods winched by pulley from the street down below.

SHOPS

Bakkerij Paul Année	10
Boekie Woekie	4
Brinkman	6
Eduard Kramer	14
Episode	7
Gerdas	8
Jan Best	9
De Kaaskamer	11
Lady Day	3
Laura Dols	5
Puccini	1
Selexyz-scheltema	13
't Winkeltje	2
Witte Tandenwinkel	12

CLUBS & VENUES

Boom Chicago	9
Café Alto	10
Carré Theatre	12
Club Home	2
Escape	3
Exit	5
Jimmy Woo	6
Melkweg (Milky Way)	7
Odeon	1
Paradiso	11
Studio 80	4
Sugar Factory	8

The Grachtengordel

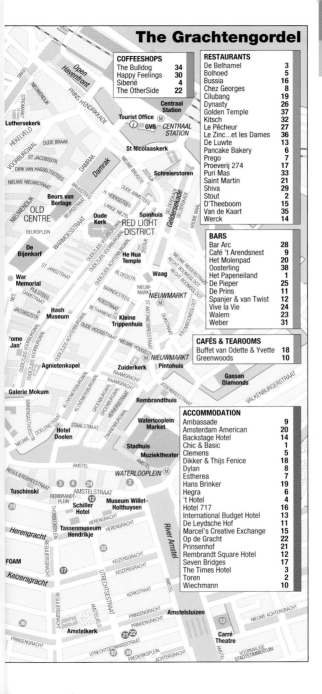

COFFEESHOPS

The Bulldog	34
Happy Feelings	30
Siberië	4
The OtherSide	22

RESTAURANTS

De Belhamel	3
Bolhoed	5
Bussia	16
Chez Georges	8
Cilubang	19
Dynasty	26
Golden Temple	37
Kitsch	32
Le Pêcheur	27
Le Zinc...et les Dames	36
De Luwte	13
Pancake Bakery	6
Prego	7
Proeverij 274	17
Puri Mas	33
Saint Martin	21
Shiva	29
Stout	2
D'Theeboom	15
Van de Kaart	35
Werck	14

BARS

Bar Arc	28
Café 't Arendsnest	9
Het Molenpad	20
Oosterling	38
Het Papeneiland	1
De Pieper	25
De Prins	11
Spanjer & van Twist	12
Vive la Vie	24
Walem	23
Weber	31

CAFÉS & TEAROOMS

Buffet van Odette & Yvette	18
Greenwoods	10

ACCOMMODATION

Ambassade	9
Amsterdam American	20
Backstage Hotel	14
Chic & Basic	1
Clemens	5
Dikker & Thijs Fenice	18
Dylan	8
Estherea	7
Hans Brinker	19
Hegra	6
't Hotel	4
Hotel 717	16
International Budget Hotel	13
De Leydsche Hof	11
Marcel's Creative Exchange	15
Op de Gracht	22
Prinsenhof	21
Rembrandt Square Hotel	12
Seven Bridges	17
The Times Hotel	3
Toren	2
Wiechmann	10

HOFJE VAN BRIENEN

Prinsengracht 85–133. Mon–Fri 6am–6pm & Sat 6am–2pm. Free. MAP PP.54–55, POCKET MAP C2

On the east side of Prinsengracht, opposite the large and conspicuous Noorderkerk (see p.74), this brown-brick courtyard was built as an almshouse in 1804 to the order of a certain Aernout van Brienen. A well-to-do merchant, Van Brienen had locked himself in his own strongroom by accident and, in a panic, he vowed to build a *hofje* if he was rescued: he was and he did. The plaque inside the complex doesn't give much of the game away, inscribed demurely with "For the relief and shelter of those in need."

LELIEGRACHT

MAP PP.54–55, POCKET MAP C3

Leliegracht leads left off Prinsengracht, and is one of the tiny radial canals that cut across the Grachtengordel. It holds one of the city's finest Art Nouveau buildings, a tall and striking building at the Leliegracht-Keizersgracht junction designed by Gerrit van Arkel in 1905. It was originally the headquarters of a life insurance company – hence the two mosaics with angels recommending policies to bemused earthlings.

THE ANNE FRANK HUIS

Prinsengracht 263 ☎ 020/556 7100, 🌐 www .annefrank.org. Daily: mid-March to June & early Sept 9am–9pm, Sat until 10pm; July & Aug 9am–10pm; mid-Sept to mid-March 9am–7pm; closed Yom Kippur. €8.50, 10- to 17-year-olds €4, under-9s free. MAP PP.54–55, POCKET MAP C3

Easily the city's most visited sight, the **Anne Frank Huis** is where the young diarist and her family hid from the Germans during World War II. Since the posthumous publication of her diaries, Anne Frank has become extraordinarily famous, in the first instance for recording the iniquities of the Holocaust, and latterly as a symbol of the fight against oppression and in particular racism. The family spent over two years in hiding here, but were eventually betrayed and dispatched to Westerbork – the transit camp in the north of the country where most Dutch Jews were processed before being moved to Belsen or Auschwitz. Of the eight souls hidden in the annexe, only Otto Frank survived; Anne and her sister died of typhus within a short

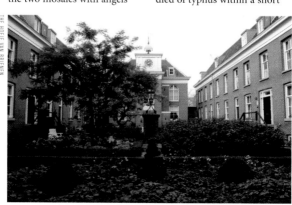

time of each other in Belsen, just one week before the German surrender.

Anne Frank's diary was among the few things left behind in the annexe. It was retrieved by one of the people who had helped the Franks and handed to Anne's father on his return from Auschwitz; he later decided to publish it. Since its appearance in 1947, it has been constantly in print and has sold millions of copies.

Despite being so popular, the house has managed to preserve a sense of intimacy, a poignant witness to the personal nature of the Franks' sufferings. The rooms the Franks occupied for two years have been left much the same as they were during the war albeit without the furniture – down to the movie star pin-ups in Anne's bedroom and the marks on the wall recording the children's heights. Video clips of the family in particular and the Holocaust in general give the background. Anne Frank was one of about 100,000 Dutch Jews who died during World War II, but this, her final home, provides one of the most enduring testaments to its horrors.

THE WESTERKERK

April–Sept: Mon–Sat 10am–5.30pm. Free.
MAP PP.54–55, POCKET MAP C3

Trapped in her house, Anne Frank liked to listen to the bells of the **Westerkerk**, just along Prinsengracht, until they were taken away to be melted down for the German war effort. The church still dominates the district, its 85-metre tower (April–Oct Mon–Sat 10am–5.30pm; €6) – without question Amsterdam's finest – soaring graciously above its surroundings. The church was designed by Hendrick de Keyser

ENTRANCE TO SECRET ANNEXE AT THE ANNE FRANK HUIS

THE GRACHTENGORDEL

and completed in 1631 as part of the general enlargement of the city, but whereas the exterior is all studied elegance, the interior is bare and plain.

WESTERMARKT

MAP PP.54–55, POCKET MAP C3

Westermarkt, an open square in the shadow of the Westerkerk, possesses two evocative memorials. At the back of the church, beside Keizersgracht, are the three pink granite triangles (one each for the past, present and future) of the **Homomonument**, the world's first memorial to persecuted gays and lesbians, commemorating all those who died at the hands of the Nazis. It was designed by Karin Daan and recalls the pink triangles the Germans made homosexuals sew onto their clothes during World War II.

Nearby, on the south side of the church by Prinsengracht, is a small but beautifully crafted **statue** of Anne Frank by the modern Dutch sculptor Mari Andriessen.

57

HUIS BARTOLOTTI

Herengracht 170–172. No public access.
MAP PP.54-55, POCKET MAP C3

A brief walk from the Westermarkt, the **Huis Bartolotti** boasts a flashy facade of red brick and stone dotted with urns and columns, faces and shells. The house is an excellent illustration of the Dutch Renaissance style, much more ornate than the typical Amsterdam canal house. The architect was Hendrick de Keyser and a director of the West India Company, Willem van den Heuvel, footed the bill. Van den Heuvel inherited a fortune from his Italian uncle and changed his name in his honour to Bartolotti – hence the name of the house.

WESTERMARKT TO LEIDSEGRACHT – THE NINE STREETS

MAP PP.54-55, POCKET MAP C3-C5

Between Westermarkt and Leidsegracht, the main canals are intercepted by a trio of cross-streets, which are themselves divided into shorter streets, collectively known as "Nine Streets", mostly named after animals whose pelts were once used in the district's tanning industry. There's Reestraat (Deer Street), Hartenstraat (Hart), Berenstraat (Bear) and Wolvenstraat (Wolf), not to mention Huidenstraat (Street of Hides) and Runstraat – a "run" being a bark used in tanning. The tanners are long gone and today these are eminently appealing shopping streets, known as De Negen Straatjes (The Nine Streets).

THE FELIX MERITIS BUILDING

Keizersgracht 324. MAP PP.54-55, POCKET MAP C4

A Neoclassical monolith of 1787, this mansion was built to house the artistic and scientific activities of the eponymous society, which was the cultural focus of the city's upper crust for nearly a hundred years. Dutch cultural aspirations did not, however, impress everyone. It's said that when Napoleon visited the city the entire building was redecorated for his reception, only to have him stalk out in disgust, claiming that the place stank of tobacco. Oddly enough, it later became the headquarters of the Dutch Communist Party, but they sold it to the council who now lease it to the Felix Meritis Foundation for experimental and avant-garde art workshops, conferences, discussions and debates.

HUIS BARTOLOTTI

LEIDSEPLEIN

THE BIJBELS MUSEUM

Herengracht 366–368 ☎ 020/624 2436,
ⓦ www.bijbelsmuseum.nl. Mon–Sat
10am–5pm, Sun 11am–5pm. €8. MAP PP.54–55,
POCKET MAP C4

The graceful and commanding
Cromhouthuizen, at
Herengracht 364–370, consist of
four matching stone mansions,
built in the 1660s for one of
Amsterdam's wealthy merchant
families, the Cromhouts, and
two of them now house the
Bijbels Museum. This contains
a splendid selection of old
Bibles, including the first
Dutch-language Bible ever
printed, dating from 1477, and a
series of idiosyncratic models of
Solomon's Temple and the
Jewish Tabernacle, plus a
scattering of archeological finds
from Palestine and Egypt.

LEIDSEPLEIN

MAP PP.54–55, POCKET MAP C5

Lying on the edge of the
Grachtengordel, **Leidseplein** is
the bustling hub of
Amsterdam's nightlife, a rather
cluttered and disorderly open
space. The square once marked
the end of the road in from
Leiden and, as horse-drawn
traffic was banned from the
centre long ago, it was here that
the Dutch left their horses and
carts – a sort of equine car
park. Today, it's quite the
opposite: continual traffic made
up of trams, bikes, cars and
pedestrians gives the place a
frenetic feel, and the
surrounding side streets are
jammed with bars, restaurants
and clubs in a bright jumble of
jutting signs and neon lights.
On a good night, Leidseplein
can be Amsterdam at its
carefree, exuberant best.

STADSSCHOUWBURG

Leidseplein 26 ☎ 020/624 2311, ⓦ www
ssba.nl. MAP PP.54–55, POCKET MAP B5

Leidseplein holds the grandiose
Stadsschouwburg, a
neo-Renaissance edifice dating
from 1894, which was so
widely criticized for its clumsy
vulgarity that the city council
of the day temporarily withheld
the money for decorating the
exterior. Home to the National
Ballet and Opera until the
Muziektheater (see p.82) was
completed on Waterlooplein in
1986, it is now used for theatre,
dance and music performances.
It also functions as the spot
where the Ajax football team
gather on the balcony to wave
to the crowds whenever they
win anything, as they often do.

LEIDSESTRAAT

MAP PP.54–55, POCKET MAP C5

Heading northeast from Leidseplein, **Leidsestraat** is a crowded shopping street that leads across the three main canals up towards the Singel and the flower market (see p.63). En route, at the corner of Keizersgracht, is the **Metz & Co** department store, which was, when it was built, the tallest commercial building in the city – one reason why the owners were able to entice Gerrit Rietveld, the leading architectural light of the De Stijl movement, to add a rooftop glass and metal showroom in 1933. The showroom has survived and is now a café offering one of the best views over the centre in this predominantly low-rise city.

THE SPIEGELKWARTIER

MAP PP.54–55, POCKET MAP C6

South of Metz & Co, along Keizersgracht, is **Nieuwe Spiegelstraat**, an appealing mixture of bookshops and corner cafés that extends south into Spiegelgracht to form the Spiegelkwartier – home to the pricey end of Amsterdam's antiques trade.

DE GOUDEN BOCHT

MAP PP.54–55, POCKET MAP D5

Nieuwe Spiegelstraat meets the elegant sweep of Herengracht near the west end of the so-called De Gouden Bocht (the **Golden Bend**), where the canal is overlooked by double-fronted mansions – some of the most opulent dwellings in the city. Most of these houses were remodelled in the late seventeenth and eighteenth centuries. Characteristically, they have double stairways leading to the entrance, underneath which the small door was for the servants, while up above, the majority of the houses are topped off by the ornamental cornices that were fashionable at the time. Classical references are common, both in form – pediments, columns and pilasters – and decoration, from scrolls and vases through to geometric patterns inspired by ancient Greece.

THE STADSARCHIEF – DE BAZEL

Vijzelstraat 32 ☎ 020/251 1800, ⓦ www .debazelamsterdam.nl. Tues–Sat 10am–5pm, Sun 11am–5pm. Free. MAP PP.54–55, POCKET MAP D5

Stretching down Vijzelstraat from Herengracht is one of

Amsterdam's most incongruous buildings – you can't possibly miss its looming, geometrical brickwork. Now home to the **Stadsarchief**, the state archives, it started out as the headquarters of a Dutch shipping company, the Nederlandsche Handelsmaatschappij, before falling into the hands of the ABN-AMRO bank, which was itself swallowed by a consortium led by the Royal Bank of Scotland in 2007. Dating to the 1920s, the building is known as **De Bazel** after the architect Karel de Bazel (1869–1923), whose devotion to theosophy – a combination of metaphysics and religious philosophy – formed and framed his design. Every facet of Bazel's building reflects the theosophical desire for order and balance from the pink and yellow brickwork of the exterior (representing male and female respectively) to the repeated use of motifs drawn from the Middle East, the source of much of the cult's spiritual inspiration. At the heart of the building is the Schatkamer (Treasury), an Art Deco extravagance that exhibits an intriguing selection of photographs and documents drawn from the city's vast archives.

THE TASSENMUSEUM HENDRIKJE (PURSE & BAG MUSEUM)

Herengracht 573 ☎ 020/524 6452, ⓦ www .tassenmuseum.nl. Daily 10am–5pm. €7.50. MAP PP.54–55, POCKET MAP E5

This delightful museum holds a superb collection of handbags, pouches, wallets, bags and purses from medieval times onwards, exhibited on three floors of a grand old mansion. The collection begins on the top floor with a curious miscellany of items from the sixteenth to the nineteenth centuries. The next floor down focuses on the twentieth century, with several beautiful Art Nouveau handbags, while the final floor is given over to temporary displays.

THE MUSEUM WILLET-HOLTHUYSEN

Herengracht 605 ☎ 020/523 1870, ⓦ www .museumwilletholthuysen.nl. Mon–Fri 10am–5pm, Sat & Sun 11am–5pm. €7. MAP PP.54–55, POCKET MAP E5

The coal-trading Holthuysen family occupied this elegant, mansion until the last of the line, Sandra Willet-Holthuysen, gifted her home and its contents to the city in 1895. The most striking room is the **Blue Room**, which has been returned to its original eighteenth-century Rococo appearance – a flashy and ornate style that the Dutch merchants regarded as the epitome of refinement and good taste. Other rooms have the more cluttered appearance of the nineteenth century and the house also displays a small collection of glass, silver, majolica and ceramics assembled by Sandra's husband, Abraham Willet.

THE AMSTEL AND THE MAGERE BRUG

MAP PP.54–55, POCKET MAP E5–G9 & F6

The Grachtengordel comes to an abrupt halt at the River Amstel. The **Magere Brug** (Skinny Bridge), spanning the Amstel at the end of Kerkstraat, is the most famous and arguably the cutest of the city's many swing bridges. Legend has it that this bridge, which dates back to about 1670, replaced an even older and skinnier version, originally built by two sisters who lived on either side of the river and were fed up with having to walk so far to see each other.

THE AMSTELSLUIZEN

MAP PP.54–55, POCKET MAP F6

The **Amstelsluizen** – or Amstel locks – are closed every night when the council begin the process of sluicing out the canals. A huge pumping station on an island out to the east of the city then starts to pump fresh water from the IJsselmeer into the canal system; similar locks on the west side of the city are left open for the surplus to flow into the IJ and, from there, out to sea. The watery content of the canals is thus regularly refreshed – though, despite this, and with three centuries of algae, prams, shopping trolleys and a few hundred rusty bikes, the water is only appealing as long as you're not actually in it.

THE AMSTELVELD AND REGULIERSGRACHT

MAP PP.54–55, POCKET MAP D5

Doubling back from the Amstel Sluizen, turn left along the north side of Prinsengracht and you soon reach the **Amstelveld**, where the Monday **flower market** sells flowers and plants, and is much less of a scrum than the Bloemenmarkt (see p.63). Adjacent

Reguliersgracht is one of the three surviving radial canals that cut across the Grachtengordel, its dainty humpback bridges and sparkling waters overlooked by charming seventeenth- and eighteenth-century canal houses.

FOAM

Keizersgracht 609 ☏ 020/551 6500, ⓦ www .foam.nl. Daily 10am–6pm, Thurs & Fri until 9pm. €8. MAP PP.54–55, POCKET MAP D5

Located right on the canal, this four-storey museum of photography breathes history on the outside, but has a modern and industrial feel once you enter. **FOAM** aims to be a platform for both well-established photographers and young and upcoming talent, providing them with an opportunity to reach a larger audience. All genres of photography are covered and exhibitions are rotated regularly, with opening days often attracting hundreds of enthusiasts. Recent exhibitions have included the abstractions of Michael Wolf, the controversial Ari Marcopoulos and Cuny Janssen's whimsical My Grandma was a Turtle.

MUSEUM VAN LOON

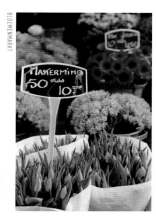

MUSEUM VAN LOON

Keizersgracht 672 ☎ 020/624 5255, ⌨ www
.museumvanloon.nl. Daily except Tues
11am–5pm. €7. MAP PP.54–55, POCKET MAP D6

The **Museum Van Loon** boasts
the finest accessible canal house
interior in Amsterdam. Built in
1672, and first occupied by the
artist and pupil of Rembrandt,
Ferdinand Bol, the house has
been returned to something
akin to its eighteenth-century
appearance, with acres of wood
panelling and fancy stucco
work. Look out also for the
ornate copper balustrade on
the staircase, into which is
worked the name "Van
Hagen-Trip" (after a one-time
owner of the house); the Van
Loons later filled the spaces
between the letters with iron
curlicues to prevent their
children falling through. The
top-floor landing has several
paintings sporting Roman
figures, and one of the
bedrooms – the "painted room"
– is decorated with a Romantic
painting of Italy, a favourite
motif in Amsterdam from
around 1750 to 1820. The
oddest items are the fake
bedroom doors: the
eighteenth-century owners
were so keen to avoid any lack
of symmetry that they
camouflaged the real bedroom
doors and created imitation,
decorative doors in the
"correct" position instead.

REMBRANDTPLEIN

MAP PP.54–55, POCKET MAP E5

One of the larger open spaces
in the city centre,
Rembrandtplein is a neat and
trim open space that was
formerly Amsterdam's butter
market. It was renamed in
1876, and is today one of the
city's nightlife centres,
although its crowded
restaurants and bars are firmly
tourist-targeted. Rembrandt's
statue stands in the middle, his
back wisely turned against the
square's worst excesses,
though, to be fair, the *Hotel
Schiller*, with its Art Deco
flourishes, does provide some
architectural flair.

THE MUNTTOREN AND BLOEMENMARKT (FLOWER MARKET)

MAP PP.54–55, POCKET MAP D5

Tiny Muntplein is dominated
by the **Munttoren**, an imposing
fifteenth-century tower that
was once part of the old city
wall. Later, the tower was
adopted as the municipal mint
– hence its name – and
Hendrik de Keyser, in one of
his last commissions, added a
flashy spire in 1620. A few
metres away, the floating
Bloemenmarkt, or **flower
market** (daily 9am–5pm, some
stalls close on Sun), extends
along the southern bank of the
Singel. Popular with locals and
tourists alike, the market is one
of the main suppliers of flowers
to central Amsterdam, but its
blooms and bulbs now share
stall space with souvenir clogs,
garden gnomes, Delftware and
similar tat.

Shops

BAKKERIJ PAUL ANNÉE

Runstraat 25. Mon–Fri 8am–6pm & Sat 8.30am–5pm. MAP PP.54–55, POCKET MAP C4

The best wholegrain and sourdough breads in town, bar none, all made from organic grains.

BOEKIE WOEKIE

Berenstraat 16. Daily noon–6pm. MAP PP.54–55, POCKET MAP C4

Sells books on – and by – leading Dutch artists and graphic designers, and entertaining postcards too.

BRINKMAN

Singel 319. Mon–Fri 10am–5pm & Sat 11am–5pm. MAP PP.54–55, POCKET MAP D4

A stalwart of the Amsterdam antiquarian book trade, *Brinkman* has lots of good local stuff with expert advice if and when you need it.

EDUARD KRAMER

Nieuwe Spiegelstraat 64. Mon–Sat 10am–6pm & Sun 1–6pm. MAP PP.54–55, POCKET MAP C6

Holds a wonderful selection of Dutch tiles from the fifteenth century onwards; it also operates an online ordering service.

EPISODE

Berenstraat 1. Mon & Sun 1–6pm, Tues–Wed 11am–6pm, Thurs 11am–8pm, Fri 11am–7pm, Sat 10am–7pm. MAP PP.54–55, POCKET MAP C4

One of the larger secondhand stores, with everything from army jackets to hats, fur coats, shoes and belts. Specializes in the 1970s and 1980s.

GERDAS

Runstraat 16. Mon–Fri 9am–6pm & Sat 9am–5pm. MAP PP.54–55 ,POCKET MAP C4

Amsterdam is full of flower shops, but this one is the most imaginative and sensual. Bouquets to melt the hardest of hearts.

JAN BEST

Keizersgracht 357, corner Huidenstraat. Mon–Fri 10.30am–6pm, Sat 10.30am–5pm & Sun 1.30–5pm. MAP PP.54–55, POCKET MAP C4

Famed antique lamp shop, with some wonderfully kitsch examples as well as offbeat new lamps and lights.

DE KAASKAMER

Runstraat 7. Mon noon–6pm, Tues–Fri 9am–6pm, Sat 9am–5pm & Sun noon–5pm. MAP PP.54–55, POCKET MAP C4

Friendly shop with a comprehensive selection of Dutch cheeses – much more than ordinary Edam – plus olives and international wines.

LADY DAY

Hartenstraat 9. Mon–Sat 11am–6pm, Thurs until 9pm & Sun 1–6pm. MAP PP.54–55, POCKET MAP C3

Good-quality secondhand clothes with the emphasis on assorted tackle from the 1950s,

LAURA DOLS

1960s and 1970s. Strong on suits and vintage dresses.

LAURA DOLS

Wolvenstraat 6 & 7. Mon–Sat 11am–6pm Thurs until 9pm & Sun 1–6pm. MAP PP.54–55, POCKET MAP C4

Superb – and superbly creative – assortment of vintage clothing from dresses through to hats. Its forte is 1940s and 1950s gear.

PUCCINI

Singel 184, junction of Oude Leliestraat, Ⓦ www.puccinibomboni.com. Mon noon–6pm, Tues–Sat 11am–6pm & Sun noon–5pm. MAP PP.54–55, POCKET MAP A11

Without doubt the best chocolatier in town, selling a wonderfully creative range of chocs in all sorts of shapes and sizes. This mini-chain has also abandoned the tweeness of the traditional chocolatier for brisk modern decor. Also at Staalstraat 17 (see p.47).

SELEXYZ-SCHELTEMA

Koningsplein 20. Mon–Sat 10am–6pm, Thurs until 9pm & Sun noon–6pm. MAP PP.54–55, POCKET MAP C5

Amsterdam's biggest and best bookshop. Six floors of absolutely everything and although most of the books are in Dutch, there are good English sections too.

'T WINKELTJE

Prinsengracht 228. Mon 1–5.30pm, Tues–Fri 10am–5.30pm & Sat 10am–5pm. MAP PP.54–55, POCKET MAP C3

A jumble of bargain-basement glassware and crockery, candlesticks, antique tin toys, kitsch souvenirs, old apothecaries' jars and flasks. Perfect for browsing.

WITTE TANDENWINKEL

Runstraat 5. Mon 1–6pm, Tues–Fri 10am–6pm & Sat 10am–5pm. MAP PP.54–55, POCKET MAP C4

The "White Teeth Shop" sells wacky toothbrushes and just about every dental hygiene accoutrement you could ever need.

Coffeeshops

THE BULLDOG

Leidseplein 15. Daily 10am–1am, 3am at weekends. MAP PP.54–55, POCKET MAP C5

The biggest and most famous of the coffeeshop chains, and a long way from its poky Red Light District-dive origins. This, the main Leidseplein branch (the Palace), housed in a former police station, has a large cocktail bar, coffeeshop, juice bar and souvenir shop, all with separate entrances. It's big and brash, not at all the place for a quiet smoke, though the dope they sell (packaged up in neat little brand-labelled bags) is reliably good.

HAPPY FEELINGS

Kerkstraat 51. Daily 1pm–1am. MAP PP.54–55, POCKET MAP C5

What used to be a hippie hangout, turned into a fresh and trendy coffeeshop with flatscreens on the walls, attracting a select clientele.

SIBERIË

Brouwersgracht 11. Sun–Thurs 11am–11pm, Fri & Sat 11am–midnight. MAP PP.54–55, POCKET MAP B10

Very relaxed, very friendly, and worth a visit whether you want to smoke or not.

THE OTHERSIDE

Reguliersdwarsstraat 6. Daily 11am–1am. MAP PP.54–55, POCKET MAP A14

Essentially a gay coffeeshop (in Dutch, "the other side" is a euphemism for gay), but straight-friendly and the atmosphere is relaxed and good fun.

Cafés and tearooms

BUFFET VAN ODETTE & YVETTE

Herengracht 309. Mon & Wed–Fri 8.30am–4.30pm, Sat 10am–5.30pm, MAP PP.54–55, POCKET MAP A13

Just walking past will get your taste buds going: a serious treat for breakfast or lunch.

GREENWOODS

Singel 103. Mon–Thurs 9.30am–6pm, Fri–Sun 9.30am–7pm. MAP PP.54–55, POCKET MAP B11

Small, English-style teashop in the basement of a canal house. Pies and sandwiches, pots of tea – and a decent breakfast.

Restaurants

DE BELHAMEL

Brouwersgracht 60 ☎ 020/622 1095. Daily 6–10pm. MAP PP.54–55, POCKET MAP B10

Smashing restaurant where the Art Nouveau decor makes for a delightful setting and the menu is short but extremely well-chosen, mixing Dutch with French dishes. Main courses at around €20–25.

BUSSIA

BOLHOED

Prinsengracht 60 ☎ 020/626 1803. Daily noon–10pm. MAP PP.54–55, POCKET MAP C2

Something of an Amsterdam institution, the daily changing menu here features familiar vegan and vegetarian options, with organic beer to wash it down. Mains at around €15.

BUSSIA

Reestraat 28 ☎ 020/627 8794. Daily noon–3pm & 6–10.30pm. MAP PP.54–55, POCKET MAP C3

Top notch Italian restaurant with fresh ingredients. Everything is homemade, from the original Italian *gelato* to the pasta. Many wines per glass. Mains around €25, a bit less for pasta.

CHEZ GEORGES

Herenstraat 3 ☎ 020/626 3332. Mon, Tues, & Thrus–Sat 6–10pm. MAP PP.54–55, POCKET MAP A11

This much-lauded restaurant offers immaculately presented dishes from a well-chosen menu. The old fashioned interior adds to the homely feel. Main courses cost €23 and up, though you might prefer the three-course set menu instead. Has an excellent selection of wines, too.

CILUBANG

Runstraat 10 ☎ 020/626 9755. Tues–Sun
6–11pm. MAP PP.54–55, POCKET MAP C4

Tiny but much-liked
Indonesian restaurant with a
friendly atmosphere, serving
spicy dishes with mains
hovering at around €20 and the
traditional *rijsttafel* from €23.

DYNASTY

Reguliersdwarsstraat 30 ☎ 020/626 8400.
Mon & Wed–Sun 5.30–10.30pm. MAP PP.54–55,
POCKET MAP A14

Offers a substantial choice of
Indochinese food, with both
Vietnamese and Thai options.
The subdued atmosphere suits
the prices, with main courses
averaging €25–30.

GOLDEN TEMPLE

Utrechtsestraat 126 ☎ 020/626 8560. Daily
5–9.30pm. MAP PP.54–55, POCKET MAP E6

Laidback place with a little
more soul than the average
Amsterdam veggie joint.
Pleasant, attentive service. No
alcohol.

KITSCH

Utrechtsestraat 42 ☎ 020/625 9251. Tues–
Sat 6–11pm. MAP PP.54–55, POCKET MAP D5

Exuberant flower power in this
retro restaurant with old
movies projected on the wall
and cushions in every thinkable
design. The menu is less
adventurous, ranging from a
simple hamburger to lobster, at
reasonable prices.

LE PÊCHEUR

Reguliersdwarsstraat 32 ☎ 020/624 3121.
Mon–Fri noon–3pm & 5.30–11pm & Sat
5.30–11pm. MAP PP.54–55, POCKET MAP A14

Seafood restaurant with a
well-considered menu, both set
menus and à la carte, with
mains around €23.

LE ZINC … ET LES DAMES

Prinsengracht 999 ☎ 020/622 9044. Mon–Sat
5.30–11pm. MAP PP.54–55, POCKET MAP D6

Atmospheric little place serving
good-quality, simple cuisine
with main courses averaging
€24; there's a good wine list too.

DE LUWTE

Leliegracht 26 ☎ 020/625 8548. Daily
6–10pm. MAP PP.54–55, POCKET MAP A11

This cordial restaurant is kitted
out with yellow tables and
pastel walls embellished with
Art Nouveau flourishes. The
small but well-chosen menu
offers Dutch/Mediterranean
cuisine – the seafood is
delicious. Mains from €20.

PANCAKE BAKERY

Prinsengracht 191 ☎ 020/625 1333. Daily
noon–9.30pm. MAP PP.54–55, POCKET MAP C2

Located in the basement of an
old canal house, this restaurant
offers a mind-boggling range
of fillings for its pancakes
(around €9).

PREGO

Herenstraat 25 ☎ 020/638 0148. Tues–Sat
6–10pm. MAP PP.54–55, POCKET MAP D2

Informal French-Mediterranean
restaurant with modern decor
offering tasty dishes such *coq au
vin, bouillabaisse* and red sea
bass with couscous. Mains €22
and up.

PANCAKE BAKERY

PROEVERIJ 274

Prinsengracht 274 ☎ 020/421 1848. Daily 5.30–10.30pm. MAP PP.54–55, POCKET MAP C4

Cosy split-level restaurant with sixteenth-century relics on the wall and a first-class menu offering classic dishes with a modern twist. Solely organic meat and fish in season. Mains from €23 and up.

PURI MAS

Lange Leidsedwarsstraat 37 ☎ 020/627 7627. Daily from 6–11pm. MAP PP.54–55, POCKET MAP C5

Exceptionally good value Indonesian, on a street better known for rip-offs. Friendly and informed service preludes spectacular *rijsttafels*, both meat and vegetarian.

SAINT MARTIN

Prinsengracht 358 ☎ 020/620 2757. Wed–Sun 4–10pm. MAP PP.54–55, POCKET MAP C5

Cheerful little place offering Mediterranean cuisine with only the freshest of ingredients in an informal setting. Attractively located on the canal side.

SHIVA

Reguliersdwarsstraat 72 ☎ 020/624 8713. Daily 5–11pm. MAP PP.54–55, POCKET MAP D5

Competent Indian restaurant in terms of quality and price, with a wide selection of dishes, all expertly prepared and moderately priced.

STOUT

Haarlemmerstraat 73 ☎ 020/616 3664. Daily 10am–11pm, Sun from 11am. MAP PP.54–55, POCKET MAP D1

Lively and fashionable café annexe restaurant, popular with locals. Great sandwiches and salads at daytime and everything from duck to fresh oysters in the evening. Comfortable velvet lounge seats outside make it a great spot to linger.

D'THEEBOOM

Singel 210 ☎ 020/623 8420. Mon–Sat 6–10pm. MAP PP.54–55, POCKET MAP C3

Traditional French restaurant in an old and attractive canal house a short walk from Dam Square. Relaxed atmosphere and attentive service. Mains from around €24.

VAN DE KAART

Prinsengracht 512 ☎ 020/625 9232. Mon–Sat 6.30–9.30pm. MAP PP.54–55, POCKET MAP C6

Slick and chic restaurant, with an excellent and enterprising French-inspired menu including such delights as poached lobster, smoked mackerel and beef cheek stew-stuffed ravioli. The selection of wines complements with vim and gusto.

WERCK

Prinsengracht 277 ☎ 020/627 4079. ⓦ www .werck.nl. Tues–Sat 5–11pm. MAP PP.54–55, POCKET MAP C3

Located right next to the Anne Frank Huis, this smart place offers flavoursome mains like pan-fried John Dory and venison stew for around €18. Turns into a lively place with DJs at night.

Bars

BAR ARC

Regulierdwarsstraat 44. Daily 4pm–1am, Fri & Sat until 3am. MAP PP.54–55, POCKET MAP D5

Huge and fashionable gay spot, with fluorescent pink lights and multiple bars. Cocktail nights and DJs on weekends. Also frequented by non-gays.

CAFÉ 'T ARENDSNEST

Herengracht 90. Daily 4pm–midnight, Fri & Sat until 2am. MAP PP.54–55, POCKET MAP D2

In a handsome old canal house, this bar boasts impressive wooden decor – from the longest of bars to the tall wood-and-glass cabinets – and specializes in Dutch beers, of which it has 130 varieties, twelve on tap.

HET MOLENPAD

Prinsengracht 653. Daily noon–1am, Fri & Sat until 2am. MAP PP.54–55, POCKET MAP C5
Café with a laidback vibe. Popular for after-work drinks.

OOSTERLING

Utrechtsestraat 140. Mon–Sat noon–1am, Sun 1–8pm. MAP PP.54–55, POCKET MAP E6
Stone-floored, neighbourhood bar-cum-off-licence that's been owned by the same family for years. Kitted out in traditional style, it specializes in *jenever* (gin) with dozens of brands and varieties.

HET PAPENEILAND

Prinsengracht 2. Daily 10am–1am, Fri & Sat until 3am. MAP PP.54–55, POCKET MAP D1
With its wood panelling, antique Delft tiles and ancient stove, this is one of the cosiest bars in the Grachtengordel, though it does get packed late at night with a garrulous crew.

DE PIEPER

Prinsengracht 424. Mon–Thurs 11am–1am, Fri & Sat until 2am. MAP PP.54–55, POCKET MAP C5
Relaxed neighbourhood brown bar with rickety old furniture and a mini-terrace beside the canal.

DE PRINS

Prinsengracht 124. Daily 10am–1am. MAP PP.54–55, POCKET MAP C3
With its well-worn decor and chatty atmosphere, this popular and lively brown bar offers a wide range of drinks and well-priced food, served 10am–10pm.

SPANJER & VAN TWIST

Leliegracht 60. Daily 10am–1am. MAP PP.54–55, POCKET MAP C2

Café-bar with an arty air and brisk modern fittings. Tasty snacks and light meals plus an outside mini-terrace right on the canal. Lunch served daily 10am–4pm, evening meals 6–10pm.

VIVE LA VIE

Amstelstraat 7. Daily 4pm–1am, Fri & Sat until 3am. MAP PP.54–55, POCKET MAP E5
Small, campy bar, patronized mostly, but not exclusively, by women and transvestites. Quiet during the week, it steams on the weekend.

WALEM

Keizersgracht 449. Daily 10am–1am, Fri & Sat until 2am. MAP PP.54–55, POCKET MAP C5
A chic café-bar – cool, light and vehemently un-brown. The clientele is stylish, and the food is hybrid Mediterranean-Eastern. Breakfast in the garden during the summer is a highlight. Usually packed.

WEBER

Marnixstraat 397. Daily 8pm–3am, Fri & Sat until 4am. MAP PP.54–55, POCKET MAP B5
Popular local hangout attracting musicians, students and young professionals. Crowded at the weekends with a friendly and amenable crew.

WEBER

Clubs and venues

BOOM CHICAGO

Leidseplein 12 ☎ 020/423 0101, Ⓦ www
.boomchicago.nl. MAP PP.54-55, POCKET MAP C5
Something of a phenomenon in
Amsterdam, this rapid-fire
improv comedy troupe hailing
from the US performs at the
Leidseplein Theater nightly to
crowds of both tourists and
locals alike. With inexpensive
food, cocktails and beer served
in pitchers, the comedy need
not be funny – but it is.

CAFÉ ALTO

Korte Leidsedwarsstraat 115 ☎ 020/626
3249, Ⓦ www.jazz-cafe-alto.nl. Daily
9pm–3am, Fri & Sat until 4am. MAP PP.54-55,
POCKET MAP C5
It's worth hunting down this
legendary little jazz bar just off
Leidseplein for its quality
modern jazz. It's big on
atmosphere, though slightly
cramped, and entry is free.

CARRÉ THEATRE

Amstel 115-125 ☎ 0900/25 25 255, Ⓦ www
.theatercarre.nl. MAP PP.54-55, POCKET MAP F6
A splendid late-nineteenth

-century structure comprises
the ultimate venue for Dutch
folk artists, and hosts all kinds
of top international acts –
anything from Van Morrison
to Carmen, with reputable
touring orchestras and opera
companies squeezed in
between.

CLUB HOME

Wagenstraat 3 ☎ 020/620 1375, Ⓦ www
.clubhome.nl. Thurs 11pm–4am, Fri & Sat
10pm–5am. Tickets € 5–12. MAP PP.54-55,
POCKET MAP E5
Relaxed dance club, divided
over three floors offering all
styles of house and club
music. Mixed audience with
mainly students on Thursday
and the hip and creative on
weekends.

ESCAPE

Rembrandtplein 11 ☎ 020/622 1111, Ⓦ www
.escape.nl. Thurs–Sun 11pm–4/5am. MAP
PP.54-55, POCKET MAP E5
This vast club has space enough
to house 2000 people, but its
glory days – when it was home
to Amsterdam's cutting edge
Chemistry nights – are long
gone and it now focuses on
weekly club nights that pull in
crowds of mainstream punters.
The opening of the *Escape* café,
lounge and studio should pull
in more trendsetting crowds
though.

EXIT

Reguliersdwarsstraat 42 ☎ 020/625 8788,
Ⓦ www.clubexit.eu. Thurs midnight–4am,
Fri & Sat midnight–5am. MAP PP.54-55, POCKET
MAP D5
A classic gay club ideally
situated for the fallout from the
surrounding nightlife, with
four bars playing different
music from R&B to house.
Attracts an upbeat, cruisey
crowd. Predominantly male,
though women are admitted.
Don't be surprised if you're

EXIT

turned away if you haven't dressed up.

JIMMY WOO

Korte Leidsedwarsstraat 18 ☎ 020/626 1181, ⓦ www.jimmywoo.com. Thurs–Sun 11pm–3/4am. MAP PP.54–55, POCKET MAP B5
Intimate and stylish club spread over two floors. Upstairs, the black lacquered walls, Japanese lamps and cosy booths with leather couches ooze sexy chic, while downstairs a packed dance floor throbs under hundreds of oscillating lightbulbs studded into the ceiling. Popular with young, well-dressed locals so look smart if you want to join in.

ODEON

MELKWEG (MILKY WAY)

Lijnbaansgracht 234a ☎ 020/531 8181, ⓦ www.melkweg.nl. MAP PP.54–55, POCKET MAP C5
Probably Amsterdam's most famous entertainment venue. A former dairy (hence the name) just round the corner from Leidseplein, this has two separate halls for live music, and puts on a broad range of bands covering everything from reggae to rock, all of which lean towards the "alternative". Excellent DJ sessions go on late at the weekend. There's also a monthly film programme, a theatre, gallery and café-restaurant (Marnixstraat entrance; Wed–Sun noon–9pm).

ODEON

Singel 460 ☎ 020/850 2420, ⓦ www.odeontheater.nl. Club Fri & Sat 11pm–5am; restaurant Fri & Sat from 6pm. MAP PP.54–55, POCKET MAP D5
Originally a brewery, this restored old canal house has since been a theatre, cinema and concert hall until it was gutted in 1990. Rescued, it's now a stylish nightclub and restaurant.

PARADISO

Weteringschans 6–8 ☎ 020/626 8790, ⓦ www.paradiso.nl. MAP PP.54–55, POCKET MAP C6
A converted church near the Leidseplein, revered by many for its excellent programme, featuring local and international bands. Club nights such as Noodlanding! draw in the crowds, and look out too for DJ sets on Saturdays. It sometimes hosts classical concerts, as well as debates and multimedia events.

STUDIO 80

Rembrandtplein 17 ☎ 020/521 8333, ⓦ www.studio-80.nl. Daily except Tues 11pm–4/5am. MAP PP.54–55, POCKET MAP E5
Right on the Rembrandtplein, this place celebrates the underground scene with techno, soul, funk, minimal and electro. A breeding ground for upcoming DJs and bands.

SUGAR FACTORY

Lijnbaansgracht 238 ☎ 020/627 0008, ⓦ www.sugarfactory.nl. Nightly except Tues & Wed. MAP PP.54–55, POCKET MAP C5
Busy Leidseplein's latest addition is the "theatrical nightclub", which hosts a programme of cabaret, live music, poetry and theatre, plus a late-night club that kicks off after the show. Pulls in a young and artistic crowd.

The Jordaan and Western docklands

On the western side of the city centre, the Jordaan is an area of slender canals and narrow streets flanked by an agreeable mix of modest, modern terraces and handsome seventeenth-century canal houses. It was traditionally the home of Amsterdam's working class, but in recent decades it has become one of the most sought-after residential neighbourhoods in the city. Until the 1970s, the inhabitants were primarily stevedores and factory workers earning a crust in the Scheepvaartsbuurt (Shipping Quarter) that edges the north of the Jordaan. This is now a mixed shopping and residential quarter, while just beyond, the Westerdok is the oldest part of the sprawling complex of artificial islands that today sweeps along the south side of the River IJ.

THE JORDAAN

MAP P.73, POCKET MAP B3

According to dyed-in-the-wool locals, the true Jordaaner is born within earshot of the Westerkerk bells, which means that there are endless arguments as to quite where the district's southern boundary lies, though at least the other borders are clear – Prinsengracht, Brouwersgracht and Lijnbaansgracht.

The streets just north of Leidsegracht – generally deemed to be the southern border – are routinely modern, but at Elandsgracht 109 you'll find the enjoyable **De Looier antiques market** (daily except Fri 11am–5pm). The area's artery, **Rozengracht**, slices through the centre, though this wide street lost most of its character when its canal was filled in and is now a busy main road of no particular distinction. It was here, at no. 184, that Rembrandt spent the last ten years of his life in diminished circumstances – a scrolled plaque distinguishes his old home.

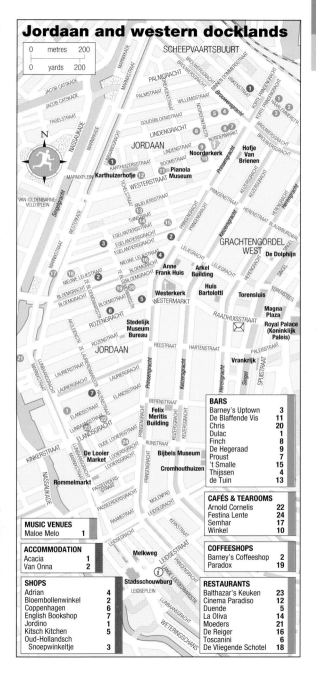

ROZENGRACHT TO WESTERSTRAAT

MAP P.73, POCKET MAP B3 & B2-C2

The streets and canals between Rozengracht and Westerstraat form the heart of the Jordaan and hold the district's prettiest sights. North of Rozengracht, the first canal is the **Bloemgracht** (Flower Canal), a leafy waterway dotted with houseboats and arched by dinky little bridges, its network of cross-streets sprinkled with cafés, bars and idiosyncratic shops. A narrow cross-street, **2e Egelantiersdwarsstraat** – and its continuation **2e Tuindwarsstraat** and **2e Anjeliersdwarsstraat** – runs north from Bloemgracht flanked by many of the Jordaan's more fashionable stores and clothing shops, as well as some of its liveliest bars and cafés. At the end is workaday **Westerstraat**, a busy modern thoroughfare dotted with more mainstream shops.

PIANOLA MUSEUM

Westerstraat 106 ☎ 020/6279624, ⊛ www .pianola.nl. Sun 2–5pm. €5. MAP P.73, POCKET MAP C2

This small but charming museum has a collection of **pianolas** and automatic music machines dating from the beginning of the twentieth century, fifteen of which have been restored to working order. These machines were the jukeboxes of their day, and the museum has a vast collection of over 15,000 rolls of music, some of which were "recorded" by famous pianists and composers – Gershwin, Debussy, Scott Joplin and others. It also runs a regular programme of pianola music concerts (exact times are on their website).

THE NOORDERKERK

Noorderkerkstraat. Mon, Thurs & Sat 11am–1pm, Wed 11am–3pm, Sun 1.30–5pm. Free. MAP P.73, POCKET MAP C2

Hendrik de Keyser's last creation, finished two years after his death in 1623, this bulky, overbearing brick building represented a radical departure from the conventional church designs of the time, having a symmetrical Greek-cross floor plan, with four equally proportioned arms radiating out from a steepled centre. Uncompromisingly dour, it proclaimed the serious intent of the Calvinists who worshipped here, its central pulpit a complete break with the Catholic past.

BLOEMGRACHT

NOORDERMARKT

MAP P.73, POCKET MAP C2

The **Noordermarkt** holds a statue of three figures bound to each other, a tribute to the bloody Jordaanoproer riot of 1934, part of a successful campaign to stop the government cutting unemployment benefit during the Depression. The square hosts some of Amsterdam's best **markets** – an antiques and household goods market on Monday mornings (9am–1pm) and the farmers' market, the **Boerenmarkt**, on Saturdays (9am–4pm).

LINDENGRACHT

MAP P.73, POCKET MAP C1

The **Lindengracht** ("Canal of Limes") lost its waterway decades ago, and is a fairly nondescript thoroughfare, though home to the Suyckerhofje of 1667 – easy to miss through a mall gateway at no. 94, and with a lovely enclosed garden that is typical of the Jordaan's many *hofjes*.

THE SCHEEPVAARTSBUURT AND THE WESTERDOK

MAP P.73, POCKET MAP C1

Brouwersgracht marks both the northern edge of the Jordaan and the southern boundary of the **Scheepvaartsbuurt** – the Shipping Quarter. In the eighteenth and nineteenth centuries, this district boomed from its location between the Brouwersgracht and the Westerdok, a narrow parcel of land dredged out of the River IJ immediately to the north and equipped with docks, warehouses and shipyards. The **Westerdok** hung on to some of the marine trade until the 1960s, but today industry has to all intents and purposes disappeared and the area is busy reinventing itself, as the old warehouses are turned into bijou studios. The nearby **Westerpark** provides a spot of green for the locals, and the restored **Westergasfabriek** some funky places to eat and drink. A five-minute walk away, under the rail tracks and left down Zaanstraat, the 1921 **Het Schip** housing development is a seminal work of the Amsterdam School and can be visited on hourly tours (Tues–Sun 11am–5pm; €7.50).

Shops

ADRIAN

Prinsengracht 130. Tues–Sat noon–6pm.
MAP P.73, POCKET MAP C3

Truly a one-off, Adrian buys fabrics from all over the world and makes them up into shirts, trousers and suits in fantastic gaudy, floral designs.

BLOEMBOLLENWINKEL

Prinsengracht 112. Daily 10am–6pm. MAP P.73,
POCKET MAP C2

Charming little shop selling packets of tulip bulbs in season. Downstairs is a small museum that charts the tulip's history from the gardens of the Ottoman Empire to becoming Amsterdam's most iconic flower.

COPPENHAGEN

Rozengracht 54. Tues–Fri 10am–6pm, Sat
10am–5pm. MAP P.73, POCKET MAP B3

Something of a Jordaan institution, this shop stocks beads and beady accessories – including everything you'll need to make your own jewellery.

ENGLISH BOOKSHOP

Lauriergracht 71. Tues–Sat 11am–6pm.
MAP P.72, POCKET MAP B4

Stocks a well-chosen collection of titles on a wide range of subjects, in particular literature.

JORDINO

Haarlemmerdijk 25a. Mon 1–7pm, Tues–Sat
10am–7pm, Sun 1–7pm. MAP P.72, POCKET MAP D1

Fantastic handmade chocolates and some of the best ice cream in the city.

KITSCH KITCHEN

Rozengracht 8. Mon–Sat 10am–6pm, Sun
noon–5pm. MAP P.72, POCKET MAP C3

Crammed full of chunky furniture and brightly coloured bowls and other home and kitchen stuff – you're bound to find something you think you need here.

OUD-HOLLANDSCH SNOEPWINKELTJE

Tweede Egelantierdwarsstraat 2. Tues–Sat
11am–6.30pm, Sun noon–5pm. MAP P.73,
POCKET MAP B2

Delicious Dutch sweets, piled up in glass jars attracting hordes of kids.

Coffeeshops

BARNEY'S COFFEESHOP

Haarlemmerstraat 102. Daily 7am–10pm.
MAP P.73, POCKET MAP D1

This popular coffeeshop is the most civilized place in town to enjoy a big hit before moving on to *Barney's Uptown* across the road for a drink.

PARADOX

1e Bloemdwarsstraat 2. Daily 10am–8pm.
MAP P.73, POCKET MAP B3

Paradox satisfies the munchies with outstanding natural food, including spectacular fresh fruit concoctions and veggie burgers.

Cafés and tearooms

ARNOLD CORNELIS

Elandsgracht 78. Mon–Fri 8.30am–6pm, Sat 8.30am–5pm. MAP P.73, POCKET MAP B4

Confectioner and patisserie with a mouth-watering display of pastries and cakes. Take away or eat in the snug tearoom.

FESTINA LENTE

Looiersgracht 40b. Mon noon–1am, Tues–Fri 10.30am–1/3am, Sat 11am–3am, Sun noon–1am. MAP P.73, POCKET MAP B4

Relaxed café-bar with armchairs to laze about on. The outside tables overlooking the canal are a suntrap in the summer.

SEMHAR

Marnixstraat 259–261 ☎ 020/638 1634. Daily 4–10pm. Closed Mon. MAP P.73, POCKET MAP D1

A small and popular Ethiopian restaurant with an authentic menu of meat, fish and veggie dishes – all mopped up with great East African flatbread. Try the African beer too, served in a *calabash* and available in a variety of exotic flavours. Large portions, and as much flatbread as you can manage. Mains from around €11.

WINKEL

Noordermarkt 43. Mon 7am–1am, Tues–Thurs 8am–1am, Fri 8am–3am, Sat 7am–3am, Sun 10am–1am. MAP P.73, POCKET MAP C2

Queue up along with the rest of Amsterdam for delectable mouthwatering apple-pie –it's homemade in this agreeable lunchroom-cum-restaurant.

Restaurants

BALTHAZAR'S KEUKEN

Elandsgracht 108 ☎ 020/420 2114. Wed–Fri from 6pm. MAP P.73, POCKET MAP B4

As the name suggests, this restaurant makes you feel like you accidentally stumbled into someone's kitchen. Their weekly changing three-course menu (€27.50) is very popular. Be sure to book.

CINEMA PARADISO

Westerstraat 186 ☎ 020/623 7344. Tues–Sun 6–11pm. MAP P.73, POCKET MAP C2

Slick place covering all the Italian classics with gusto. It's in a former moviehouse and very popular, so you may have to shout to be heard. Pasta and pizzas from €12.

DUENDE

Lindengracht 62 ☎ 020/420 6692. Mon–Thurs 5pm–1am, Fri & Sat 4pm–3am, Sun 4pm–1am. Kitchen until 11pm. MAP P.73, POCKET MAP C1

Busy tapas bar with a tiled interior and a warm and inviting feel. Good food, and there's also a small venue that hosts flamenco at weekends.

LA OLIVA

Egelantiersstraat 122 ☎ 020/320 4316. Daily except Tues noon–10.30pm. MAP P.73, POCKET MAP B2

This sleek Jordaan eatery specializes in *pinxtos*, the delectable Basque snacks-on-sticks that make Spanish bar-hopping such a delight.

TAPAS

MOEDERS

Rozengracht 251 ☎ 020/626 7957. Daily 5–10.30pm. MAP P.73, POCKET MAP B3
Really cosy restaurant just across from the Singelgracht whose theme is obvious the moment you walk in – mothers, photos of thousands of whom plaster the walls. Food is predictably homespun Dutch grub with the odd modern twist, very tasty and reasonably priced.

DE REIGER

Nieuwe Leliestraat 34 ☎ 020/624 7426. Tues–Thurs & Sun 5pm–midnight. Fri 5pm–1am, Sat 3pm–1am. MAP P.73, POCKET MAP C3

In the thick of the Jordaan, this is an old-style café filled with modish Amsterdammers. Dinner around €19.

TOSCANINI

Lindengracht 75 ☎ 020/623 2813. Mon–Sat 6–10.30pm. MAP P.73, POCKET MAP C1
Big, bustling and very authentic Italian restaurant, with great daily specials and an extensive and delicious wine list of regional Italian wines. Excellent service and a nice atmosphere.

DE VLIEGENDE SCHOTEL

Nieuwe Leliestraat 162 ☎ 020/625 2041. Daily 5–9.30pm. MAP P.73, POCKET MAP B3
Perhaps the pick of the city's cheap and wholesome vegetarian restaurants, the "Flying Saucer" serves delicious food in large portions. Mains are around €12.

Bars

BARNEY'S UPTOWN

Haarlemmerstraat 105. Daily 8am–1am, Fri & Sat until 3am. MAP P.73, POCKET MAP D1
Pleasant, smoker-friendly bar that's the slick night-time sister of the coffeeshop across the street (see p.76), with DJs providing a humming backdrop. The American(ish) menu has a good choice of burgers, steaks and sandwiches, and they also specialize in huge breakfasts and weekend brunch.

DE BLAFFENDE VIS

Westerstraat 118. Daily 9am–1am, Mon from 7am, Fri & Sat until 3am. MAP P.73, POCKET MAP C2
Somewhat of an institution, this typical neighbourhood bar sits at the corner of the 2e Boomdwarsstraat. Nothing pretentious, but oodles of atmosphere and a well-priced bar menu.

CHRIS

Bloemstraat 42. Daily 3pm–1am, Fri & Sat until 2am, Sun until 9pm. MAP P.73, POCKET MAP B3
This place is very proud of itself for being the Jordaan's (and Amsterdam's) oldest bar –it dates from 1624. The atmosphere is homely and cosy.

FINCH

DULAC

Haarlemmerstraat 118. Mon & Tues from 4pm, Wed–Sun from noon. MAP P.73, POCKET MAP D1

An appealing Art Deco grand café housed in what was an old city bank. The metal cage doors remain but now the only money changing hands is at the bar, especially on weekends when it stays open till 3am.

FINCH

Noordermarkt 5. Daily 10am–1am, Fri & Sat until 3am. MAP P.73, POCKET MAP C1

This smart café-lounge bar situated near the Noorderkerk attracts a stylish crowd, who come here to enjoy the design-school ambience, good tunes and superb location. Lunch from noon, dinner from 6pm.

DE HEGERAAD

Noordermarkt 34. Daily 8am–1am, Fri & Sat until 3am, Sun from 11am. MAP P.73, POCKET MAP C2

Lovingly maintained brown café with a loyal clientele. The back room is the perfect place to relax with a hot chocolate.

PROUST

Noordermarkt 4. Mon 9am–1am, Tues–Thurs noon–1am, Fri noon–3am, Sat 9.30am–3am, Sun noon–1am. MAP P.73, POCKET MAP C1

Trendy bar with a laidback Jordaan atmosphere, attracting students and young urban professionals. Reasonably priced bar menu and drinks.

'T SMALLE

Egelantiersgracht 12. Daily 10am–1am, Fri & Sat until 2am. MAP P.73, POCKET MAP C2

Candle-lit and comfortable, this is one of Amsterdam's oldest cafés: it opened in 1786 as a tasting house for the (long-gone) gin distillery next door.

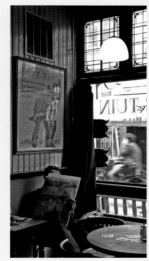

DE TUIN

THIJSSEN

Brouwersgracht 107. Mon–Thurs 8am–1am, Fri 8am–3am, Sat 7.30am–3am, Sun 9am–1am. MAP P.73, POCKET MAP C1

An old-time favourite with neighbourhood locals. Nothing fancy, but perfect to linger over coffee or fresh mint tea with a magazine.

DE TUIN

2e Tuindwarsstraat 13. Daily 10am–1am, Fri & Sat until 3am, Sun from 11am. MAP P.73, POCKET MAP C2

The Jordaan has some marvellously unpretentious bars, and this is one of the best: unkempt and always filled with locals.

Music venues

MALOE MELO

Lijnbaansgracht 163 ☎ 020/420 4592, ✆ www .maloemelo.nl. MAP P.73, POCKET MAP B4

Dark, low-ceilinged bar, with a small back room featuring local blues acts. Jam sessions take place Sunday to Thursday.

The Old Jewish Quarter and Eastern docklands

The narrow slice of land sandwiched between the curve of the River Amstel, Oudeschans and the Nieuwe Herengracht was the home of Amsterdam's Jews from the sixteenth century up until World War II. By the 1920s, this Old Jewish Quarter, or the Jodenhoek ("Jews' Corner"), was crowded with tenement buildings and smoking factories, its main streets holding scores of open-air stalls selling everything from pickled herrings to pots and pans. The war put paid to all this. In 1945 it lay derelict, and neither has postwar redevelopment treated it kindly; new building has robbed the district of much of its character. But persevere: among the cars and concrete around Waterlooplein and Mr Visserplein are several moving reminders of the Jewish community that perished in the war, while the neighbouring residential area of Plantagebuurt is home to the Artis Zoo and the excellent Verzetsmuseum (Dutch Resistance Museum). From here it's a short hop north to Oosterdok, where pride of place goes to the Nederlands –Scheepvaartmuseum (Maritime Museum), though this is currently closed for redevelopment.

THE REMBRANDTHUIS

THE REMBRANDTHUIS

Jodenbreestraat 4 ☏ 020/520 0400,
Ⓦ www.rembrandthuis.nl. Daily 10am–5pm.
€9. MAP PP.82-83, POCKET MAP E4

St Antoniesbreestraat runs into Jodenbreestraat, the "Broad Street of the Jews", which was once the main centre of Jewish activity. This ancient thoroughfare is short on charm, but it is home to the **Rembrandthuis**, whose intricate facade is decorated with pretty wooden shutters. Rembrandt bought this house at the height of his fame and popularity, living here for over twenty years and spending a fortune on furnishings – an expense that ultimately contributed to his bankruptcy. An inventory made at the time details the huge collection of paintings, sculptures and art treasures he'd amassed, almost all of which was auctioned off after he was declared insolvent and forced to move to a more modest house in the Jordaan in 1658.

The city council bought the Jodenbreestraat house in 1907 and has revamped the premises on several occasions, most recently in 1999. A visit begins in the modern building next door, but you're soon into the string of period rooms that have been returned to something like their appearance when Rembrandt lived here, with the inventory as a guide. The period furniture is enjoyable enough, especially the box-beds, and the great man's studio is surprisingly large and well-lit, but there are no Rembrandt paintings on display except when there are special exhibitions (for which expect to pay extra). However, the museum possesses an extensive collection of Rembrandt's etchings and prints as well as several of the original copper plates on which he worked, and these are on display when temporary exhibitions allow. To see more of Rembrandt's paintings, head for the Rijksmuseum (see p.95).

GASSAN DIAMONDS

Nieuwe Uilenburgerstraat 173 ☏ 020/622
5333, Ⓦ www.gassandiamonds.nl. Frequent 1hr
guided tours daily 9am–5pm. Free; no advance
booking required. MAP PP.82-83, POCKET MAP F4

Gassan Diamonds occupies a large and imposing brick building dating from 1897. Before World War II, many local Jews worked as diamond cutters and polishers, but there's little sign of the industry hereabouts today, this factory being the main exception. Tours include a visit to the cutting and polishing areas, as well a gambol round Gassan's diamond jewellery showroom.

THE STADHUIS EN MUZIEKTHEATER

Box office ☎ 020/625 5455, ⓦ www
.het-muziektheater.nl. MAP PP.82–83,
POCKET MAP E5

Jodenbreestraat runs parallel to the **Stadhuis en Muziektheater**, a sprawling and distinctly underwhelming modern complex dating from the 1980s and incorporating the city hall and a large auditorium. The Muziektheater offers a varied programme of theatre, dance and ballet as well as opera from the country's first-rate Netherlands Opera (De Nederlandse Opera; ⓦ www.dno.nl), but tickets go very quickly. One of the city's abiding ironies is that the title of the protest campaign aiming to prevent the development in the 1980s – "Stopera" – has passed into common usage to describe the finished item. Inside, amid all the architectural mediocrity, there are a couple of minor attractions, beginning with the glass columns in the public passageway towards the rear of the complex. These give a salutary lesson on the fragility of the Netherlands: two columns contain water indicating the sea levels in the Dutch towns of Vlissingen and IJmuiden (below knee height), while another records the levels experienced during the 1953 flood disaster (way above head height). At their base, a concrete pile shows what is known as "Normal Amsterdam Level" (NAP), originally calculated in 1684 as the average water level in the river IJ and still the basis for measuring altitude above sea level across Europe.

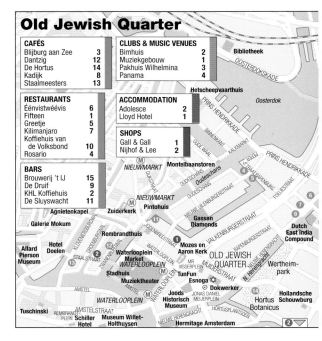

Old Jewish Quarter

CAFÉS	
Blijburg aan Zee	3
Dantzig	12
De Hortus	14
Kadijk	8
Staalmeesters	13

RESTAURANTS	
Éénvistwéévis	6
Fifteen	1
Greetje	5
Kilimanjaro	7
Koffiehuis van de Volksbond	10
Rosario	4

BARS	
Brouwerij 't IJ	15
De Druif	9
KHL Koffiehuis	2
De Sluyswacht	11

CLUBS & MUSIC VENUES	
Bimhuis	2
Muziekgebouw	1
Pakhuis Wilhelmina	3
Panama	4

ACCOMMODATION	
Adolesce	2
Lloyd Hotel	1

SHOPS	
Gall & Gall	1
Nijhof & Lee	2

WATERLOOPLEIN

MAP PP.82–83, POCKET MAP E5–F5

The indeterminate modernity of the Stadhuis complex dominates **Waterlooplein**, a rectangular parcel of land that was originally swampy marsh. This was the site of the first Jewish Quarter, but by the late nineteenth century it had become an insanitary slum. The slums were cleared in the 1880s and thereafter the open spaces of the Waterlooplein hosted the largest and liveliest market in the city, the place where Jews and Gentiles met to trade. In the war, the Germans used the square to round up their victims, but despite these ugly connotations the Waterlooplein was revived in the 1950s as the site of the city's main **flea market** (Mon–Sat 9am–5pm) and remains so to this day. It's nowhere near as large as it once was, but nonetheless it's still the final resting place of many a pair of yellow corduroy flares and has some wonderful antique and junk stalls to root through – and secondhand vinyl too. If you're after a bargain or two, head there early, as it's very popular with tourists.

Nearby, at the very tip of Waterlooplein, where the River Amstel meets the Zwanenburgwal canal, there is a sombre **memorial** – a black stone tribute to the dead of the Jewish resistance. The inscription from Jeremiah translates, "If my eyes were a well of tears, I would cry day and night for the fallen fighters of my beloved people."

THE ESNOGA

MR VISSERPLEIN

MAP PP.82–83, POCKET MAP F4

Just behind the Muziek-theater, on the corner of **Mr Visserplein**, is the **Mozes en Aaron Kerk**, a rather glum Neoclassical structure built on the site of a clandestine Catholic church in the 1840s. The square itself, a busy junction for traffic speeding towards the IJ tunnel, takes its name from Mr Visser, President of the Supreme Court of the Netherlands in 1939. He was dismissed the following year when the Germans occupied the country, and became an active member of the Jewish resistance, working for the illegal underground newspaper *Het Parool* ("The Password") and refusing to wear the yellow Star of David. He died in 1942, a few days after publicly – and famously – denouncing all forms of collaboration.

THE ESNOGA

Mr Visserplein ⓦ www.esnoga.com. April–Oct Sun–Fri 10am–4pm; Nov–March Sun–Thurs 10am–4pm & Fri 10am–2pm; closed Yom Kippur. €6.50. MAP PP.82–83, POCKET MAP F5

The brown and bulky brickwork of the **Esnoga** or Portuguese synagogue was completed in 1675 for the city's Sephardic community. One of Amsterdam's most imposing buildings, it has been barely altered since its construction, its lofty interior following the Sephardic tradition in having the *Hechal* (the Ark of the Covenant) and *tebah* (from where services are led) at opposite ends. Also traditional is the seating, with two sets of wooden benches (for the men) facing each other across the central aisle – the women have separate galleries up above. A set of superb brass chandeliers holds the candles that remain the only source of artificial light. When it was completed, the synagogue was one of the largest in the world, its congregation almost certainly the richest; today, the Sephardic community has dwindled to just 250 families, most of whom live outside the city centre. In one of the outhouses, a video sheds light on the history of the synagogue and Amsterdam's Sephardim. The mystery is why the Nazis left the building alone – no one knows for sure, but it seems likely that they intended to turn it into a museum once all the Jews had been polished off.

TUNFUN

Mr Visserplein 7 ☎ 020/689 4300, ⓦ www
.tunfun.nl. Daily 10am–6pm. €7.50, free
for adults and under-1s. MAP PP.82–83,
POCKET MAP F5

This large **indoor playground**
near the Portuguese synagogue
for children aged 1–12, has lots
of equipment to clamber into,
under and over, and a host of
activities and workshops
including football, gymnastics,
films and trampolining.
Children must be accompanied
by an adult, and there's a café
to sit in if you feel you've
already been in one ball park
too many.

JONAS DANIEL MEIJERPLEIN

MAP PP.82–83, POCKET MAP F5

Jonas Daniel Meijerplein was
where, in February 1941,
around 400 Jewish men were
forcibly loaded up on trucks
and taken to their deaths at
Mauthausen concentration
camp, in reprisal for the killing
of a Dutch Nazi during a street
fight. The arrests sparked off the
February Strike, a general strike
in protest against the Germans'
treatment of the Jews. It was
organized by the outlawed
Communist Party and
spearheaded by Amsterdam's
transport workers and dockers
– a rare demonstration of
solidarity with the Jews, whose
fate was usually accepted
without visible protest in all of
occupied Europe. The strike
was quickly suppressed, but is
still commemorated by an
annual wreath-laying ceremony
on February 25, as well as by
Mari Andriessen's statue *The
Dokwerker* (Dockworker)
standing on the square.

JOODS HISTORISCH MUSEUM

Nieuwe Amstelstraat 1 ☎ 020/531 0310,
ⓦ www.jhm.nl. Daily 11am–5pm; closed Yom
Kippur. €9. MAP PP.82–83, POCKET MAP F5

The **Joods Historisch Museum**
– Jewish Historical Museum –
is cleverly shoehorned into four
adjacent Ashkenazi synagogues
that date back to the late
seventeenth century. For many
years after the war these
buildings lay abandoned, but
they were refurbished – and
connected by walkways – in the
1980s to accommodate a Jewish
resource centre and exhibition
area. Renovations have given
the museum more space to
host some splendid temporary
exhibitions in the New
Synagogue, as well as an
overview of the more recent
history of Jews in the
Netherlands divided into three
periods – pre-, during and
postwar. The highlight of a visit
is the display on Jewish religion
and traditions until 1900,
exhibited in the main body of
the handsome **Grote
Synagogue**, which includes a
collection of religious
silverware as well as some
paintings, plus all manner of
antique artefacts illustrating
religious practices. The third
synagogue open to the public,
Obbene Sjoel, has been turned
into a multi-level children's
museum giving them an insight
in the Jewish way of living.

JOODS HISTORISCH MUSEUM

HERMITAGE

Amstel 51 ☎ 020/530 7488, Ⓦ www
.hermitage.nl. Daily 10am–5pm, Wed till 8pm.
€15. MAP PP.82–83, POCKET MAP F5

In 2004, the renowned
Hermitage museum in
St Petersburg opened its first
foreign branch here in
Amsterdam, a result of the
close cooperation between the
museum and Amsterdam's
Nieuwe Kerk. With some three
million items, the Hermitage is
Russia's leading art museum,
possessing an extensive
collection of medieval and
early modern paintings as
well as oriental art and
Post-Impressionist work.
Initially, small parts of the
Hermitage collection were
shown in Amsterdam during
temporary exhibitions and
these proved so popular that
they inspired a much larger
project: the **Amstelhof**, a large
former nursing home built
between 1681 and 1683, and
that had lain empty for many
years, was redeveloped at great
cost to house material loaned
by the Hermitage. The
Amstelhof now provides the
Hermitage with over 4000
square metres of exhibition
space, quite enough to house a
string of prestigious temporary
displays.

THE PLANTAGEBUURT

MAP PP.82–83, POCKET MAP G5–H5

Developed in the middle of the
nineteenth century, the
Plantagebuurt, with its
comfortable streets spreading
to either side of the Plantage
Middenlaan boulevard, was
built as part of a concerted
attempt to provide
good-quality housing for the
city's expanding middle classes.
Although it was never as
fashionable as the older
residential parts of the
Grachtengordel (see p.52–71),
the new district did contain
elegant villas and spacious
terraces, making it a first
suburban port of call for many
aspiring Jews. Nowadays, the
Plantagebuurt is still one of the
more prosperous parts of the
city, in a modest sort of way,
and boasts two especially
enjoyable attractions – the
Hortus Botanicus botanical
gardens and the
Verzetsmuseum (Dutch
Resistance Museum).

HORTUS BOTANICUS

Plantage Middenlaan 2a ☎ 020/625 9021,
Ⓦ www.dehortus.nl. Mon–Fri 9am–5pm, Sat &
Sun 10am–5pm; closes 4pm in Dec & Jan,
open until 7pm in July & Aug. €7.50. MAP
PP.82–83, POCKET MAP F5–G4

Amsterdam's lush **Hortus
Botanicus** were founded in
1682 as medicinal gardens for
the use of the city's physicians
and apothecaries. Thereafter,
many of the city's merchants
made a point of bringing back
exotic species from the East,
the result being the 6000-odd
plant species exhibited today.
The gardens are divided into
several distinct sections, each
clearly labelled and its location
pinpointed by a map available
at the entrance kiosk.

Most of the outdoor sections
are covered by plants, trees and
shrubs from the temperate and
Arctic zones. There's also a
three-climates glasshouse,
where the plants are arranged
according to their geographical
origins, a capacious palm
house, an orchid nursery and a
butterfly house. It's all very
low-key – and none the worse
for that – and the gardens
make a relaxing break on any
tour of central Amsterdam,
especially as the café, in the old
orangery, serves up tasty
sandwiches, coffee and cakes
(see p.91).

HORTUS BOTANICUS

WERTHEIMPARK

MAP PP.82–83, POCKET MAP G4

The pocket-sized **Wertheimpark**, across the road from the Hortus Botanicus, is home to the Auschwitz Monument, a simple affair with symbolically broken mirrors and an inscription that reads *Nooit meer Auschwitz* ("Auschwitz – Never Again"). It was designed by the late Dutch writer Jan Wolkers.

DE HOLLANDSCHE SCHOUWBURG

Plantage Middenlaan 24 ⓦ www .hollandscheschouwburg.nl. Daily 11am–4pm; closed Yom Kippur. Free. MAP PP.82–83, POCKET MAP G5

Another sad relic of the war, **De Hollandsche Schouwburg** was once a thriving Jewish theatre, but the Nazis turned it into the main assembly point for Amsterdam Jews prior to their deportation. Inside, there was no daylight and families were interned in conditions that foreshadowed those of the camps they would soon be taken to. The building has been refurbished to house a small exhibition on the plight of the city's Jews, but the old auditorium out at the back has been left as an empty, roofless shell. A memorial column of basalt on a Star of David base stands where the stage once was, an intensely mournful monument to suffering of unfathomable proportions.

ARTIS ZOO

Plantage Kerklaan 38–40 ☎ 020/523 3481. ⓦ www.artis.nl. Daily: April–Oct 9am–6pm; Nov–March 9am–5pm; June–Aug Sat until dusk. €18.50; 3- to 9-year-olds €15. MAP PP.82–83, POCKET MAP G5

Opened in 1838, **Artis Zoo** is the oldest zoo in the Netherlands and one of the city's top tourist attractions, though thankfully its layout and refreshing lack of bars and cages mean that it never feels overcrowded. Highlights include an African savanna environment, a seventy-metre-long aviary, aquaria and a South American zone with llamas and the world's largest rodent, the capybara. Feeding times – always popular – include 10.30am for the birds of prey; 11.30am and 3.45pm seals and sea lions; 2pm pelicans; 12.30pm crocodiles (Sun only); 3pm lions and tigers (not Thurs); and 3.30pm penguins. In addition, the on-site Planetarium has five or six shows daily, all in Dutch, though you can pick up a leaflet with an English translation from the desk.

VERZETSMUSEUM

Plantage Kerklaan 61 ☏ 020/620 2535, ⊛ www.verzetsmuseum.org, Mon, Sat & Sun 11am–5pm, Tues–Fri 10am–5pm, €7.50. MAP PP.82–83, POCKET MAP G5

The excellent **Verzetsmuseum** (Dutch Resistance Museum) outlines the development of the Dutch Resistance from the German invasion of the Netherlands in May 1940 to the country's liberation in 1945. The central gangway examines the main themes of the occupation, dealing honestly with the fine balance between cooperation and collaboration, while smaller displays to either side are devoted to different aspects of the resistance, from the Communist-led protest against the rounding-up of Amsterdam's Jews in 1941, to the so-called Milk Strike of 1943. There are fascinating old photographs and a host of original artefacts including examples of illegal newsletters and signed German death warrants. Apart from the treatment of the Jews, which is detailed here, perhaps the most chilling feature of the occupation was the use of indiscriminate reprisals to terrify the population. The museum also has dozens of little metal sheets providing biographical sketches of the members of the Resistance.

THE OOSTERDOK

MAP PP.82–83, POCKET MAP H3–H4

Just to the north of the Plantagebuurt lies the **Oosterdok**, whose network of artificial islands was dredged out of the River IJ to increase Amsterdam's shipping facilities in the seventeenth century. By the 1980s, this mosaic of docks, jetties and islands had become something of a post-industrial eyesore, but since then an ambitious redevelopment programme has turned things around. Easily the most agreeable way of reaching the Oosterdok is via the footbridge at the north end of Plantage Kerklaan – and metres from the Verzetsmuseum – which leads onto Entrepotdok.

ENTREPOTDOK

MAP PP.82–83, POCKET MAP G4–G5

Over the footbridge at the end of Plantage Kerklaan lies one of the more interesting of the Oosterdok islands, a slender rectangle whose southern quayside, **Entrepotdok**, is lined by a long series of nineteenth-century gabled warehouses that were once part of the largest warehouse

NEMO

complex in continental Europe. Above the main entrance, each warehouse sports the name of a town or island; goods for onward transportation were stored in the appropriate warehouse until there were enough to fill a boat or barge. The warehouses have been converted into offices and apartments, a fate that must surely befall the buildings of the central East India Company compound, at the west end of Entrepotdok on Kadijksplein.

THE NEDERLANDS SCHEEPVAARTMUSEUM

Kattenburgerplein 1 ☎ 020/523 2222, ⓦ www.scheepvaartmuseum.nl. MAP PP.82–83, POCKET MAP G4

From Kadijksplein, it's a brief walk over to the **Nederlands Scheepvaartmuseum** (Netherlands Maritime Museum), which occupies the old arsenal of the Dutch navy, a vast sandstone structure that is underpinned by no less than 18,000 wooden piles driven deep into the river bed at enormous expense in the 1650s. At the time of writing, the museum is closed for renovation, and is expected to re-open by the end of 2013. The full-scale replica of an East Indiaman, *the Amsterdam*, can still be visited though, and is moored near the

NEMO centre, a short walk from the museum.

ARCAM

Prins Hendrikkade 600 ☎ 020/620 4878, ⓦ www.arcam.nl. Tues–Sat 1–5pm. Free. MAP PP.82–83, POCKET MAP G4

Strolling west from the Maritime Museum along the waterfront, you'll soon spy the idiosyncratic hood-shaped structure that has been built to house the Amsterdam Centre for Architecture, **ARCAM**. It hosts architectural displays, sometimes of a theoretical nature and sometimes warning/informing the city of what is in the architectural pipeline. There are also public lectures and discussions hosted here.

NEMO

Prins Hendrikkade ☎ 020/531 3233, ⓦ www.e-nemo.nl. Tues–Sun 10am–5pm, plus Mon 10am–5pm during school hols and June–Aug. €12.50. MAP PP.82–83, POCKET MAP G3

Back outside the ARCAM building, the foreground is dominated by a massive elevated hood that rears up above the entrance to the IJ tunnel. A good part of this is occupied by the large and lavish **NEMO** centre, a (pre-teenage) kids' attraction par excellence, with all sorts of interactive science and technological exhibits spread over six floors and set out under several broad themes.

THE MUZIEKGEBOUW

Piet Heinkade 1 ☎ 020/788 2010. No fixed
opening times – open for performances.
MAP PP.82-83, POCKET MAP G2

One of the Eastern dockland's
prime buildings, the
Muziekgebouw is a brand-new,
high-spec, multipurpose music
auditorium overlooking the
River IJ. It encompasses two
medium-sized concert halls,
a café and a bar. It also has
state-of-the-art acoustics,
and has given real impetus to
the redevelopment going on
along the IJ. As well as some
contemporary music, it has a
good programme of opera and
orchestral music which brings a
rather highbrow crowd to this
part of town – and it's worth a
visit for the building alone.

ZEEBURG

MAP PP.82-83, POCKET MAP A3

To the north and east of the
Oosterdok, **Zeeburg** – basically
the old docklands between the
city library and **KNSM Island**
– has become one of the city's
most up-and-coming districts.
Actually a series of artificial
islands and peninsulas
connected by bridges, the
docks here date back to the end
of the nineteenth century. By
the early 1990s, the area was
virtually derelict so the city
council began a massive

renovation, which has been
going on for the past fifteen
years or so. As a result, this is
the fastest-developing part of
Amsterdam, with a mixture of
renovated dockside structures
and new landmark buildings
that give it a modern (and very
watery) feel that's markedly
different from the city centre –
despite beginning just a
ten-minute walk from Centraal
Station. Explore the area by
bike, especially as distances are,
at least in Amsterdam terms,
comparatively large – from the
library to the east end of
KNSM Island is about 4km.

Alternatively, there are two
useful transport connections
from Centraal Station: tram
#26 to Sporenburg island via
Piet Heinkade and bus #42 to
Java Island and KNSM Island.

NEDERLANDS PERSMUSEUM

Zeeburgerkade 10. ☎ 020/692 8810, ⓦ www
.persmuseum.nl. Tues–Fri 10am–5pm & Sun
noon–5pm. €4.50. MAP PP.82-83.

From the west end of Borneo
island to the south of KNSM
Island, C van Eesterenlaan
slices south across a wide strip
of water, the old Entrepothaven,
bound for Zeeburgerkade,
which is home to the
Nederlands Persmuseum. The
museum has a mildly
interesting series of displays on
the leading Dutch
newspapermen of yesteryear,
beginning with Abraham
Casteleyn, who first published a
combined business and political
newssheet in the 1650s.

Of more immediate interest
perhaps are the cartoons, often
vitriolic attacks on those in
power both in the Netherlands
and elsewhere; for instance,
the last premier – Jan Peter
Balkenende – is often
mockingly portrayed as Harry
Potter (he looks like him).

THE MUZIEKGEBOUW

Shops

GALL & GALL

Jodenbreestraat 23. Mon 11am–9pm, Tues–Sat 10am–9pm, Sun 11am–8pm. MAP PP.82–83, POCKET MAP F4

Has an outstanding range of Dutch *jenevers* (gins) and flavoured spirits as well as a good selection of imported wines. Part of a popular chain.

NIJHOF & LEE

Staalstraat 13a. Mon noon–6pm, Tues–Sat 10am–6pm & Sun noon–6pm. MAP PP.82–83, POCKET MAP E4

One of the city's best art bookshops, it stocks a raft of English-language titles and is good for photography too. Mostly new books, but some rare and antique ones as well.

Cafés

BLIJBURG AAN ZEE

Muider laar 1001. Opening hours vary according to weather conditions. MAP PP.82–83, POCKET MAP H3

Amsterdam's own city beach situated on the IJsselmeer. The beach might be somewhat of a disappointment, but *Blijburg* is very much happening with DJs in summer and live music in winter. Last stop of tram #26 from Centraal Station.

DANTZIG

Zwanenburgwal 15. Daily 9am–10pm, Sat & Sun from 10am. MAP PP.82–83, POCKET MAP E4

Easy-going grand café, right next to the Muziektheater. Comfortable chairs, friendly service and a low-key, chic atmosphere. The kitchen is open all day, except for a brief break 5–6pm.

DE HORTUS

Plantage Middenlaan 2a. Mon–Fri 9am–4.30pm, Sat & Sun 10am–4.30pm; Dec

DE HORTUS

& Jan closes 3.30pm; July & Aug until 8.30pm. MAP PP.82–83, POCKET MAP F5

The café in the orangery of the Hortus Botanicus (see p.86) serves tasty sandwiches and rolls plus the best blueberry cheesecake in the Western world. You do have to pay to get into the gardens to get to the café.

KADIJK

Kadijksplein 5. Mon 6–10pm. Tues–Sun noon–10pm. MAP PP.82–83, POCKET MAP G4

Tiny place which – contrary to what the homely interior with Delft blue crockery might suggest – has an excellent Indonesian inspired menu. Tasty *saté, soto ajam* and traditional Indonesian *spekkoek* (spiced cake) served with coffee.

STAALMEESTERS

Kloveniersburgwal 127. Daily 10am–10.30pm. MAP PP.82–83, POCKET MAP E4

Cosy if cramped café, with wooden tables and a big replica of Rembrandt's *Staalmeesters* on the wall. Breakfast until 4.30pm for the genuine night crawler and a small selection of cocktails.

Restaurants

ÉÉNVISTWÉÉVIS

Schippersgracht 61 ☎ 020/623 2894. Tues–
Sun 6–10pm. MAP PP.82-83, POCKET MAP G4

An uncomplicated fish
restaurant serving an interesting
selection of seafood, such as
seabass with rosemary and
thyme. Mains at around €23.

FIFTEEN

Jollemanshof 9 ☎ 020/509 5015. Daily
noon–3pm & 6–10pm. MAP PP.82-83, POCKET MAP H2

The Amsterdam branch of
Jamie Oliver's successful
formula, annually giving a
bunch of youngsters the chance
to prove themselves in a
top-notch restaurant. Also a
less formal trattoria and lounge.

GREETJE

Peperstraat 23 ☎ 020/779 7450. Tues–Sun
5–10pm, Sat until 11pm. MAP PP.82-83, POCKET
MAP F4

A cosy, busy restaurant that
serves up Dutch staples with a
modern twist. A changing
menu reflects the seasons and
the favourite dishes of the
owner's mother – a native of
the southern Netherlands.
Superb home-cooking in a
great atmosphere.

GREETJE

KILIMANJARO

Rapenburgerplein 6 ☎ 020/622 3485. Tues–
Sun 5–10pm. MAP PP.82-83, POCKET MAP G4

African restaurant in a largely
forgotten part of town, serving
West African antelope goulash,
Moroccan *tajine* and crocodile
steak. Vegetarian options
available. Small, moderately
priced and super-friendly.

KOFFIEHUIS VAN DE VOLKSBOND

Kadijksplein 4 ☎ 020/622 1209. Mon–Sat
6–10pm, Sun 5–9pm. MAP PP.82-83,
POCKET MAP G4

Formerly a Communist Party
café and apparently the place
where the local dockworkers
used to receive their wages,
this is now an Oosterdok
café-restaurant – try the
sauerkraut.

ROSARIO

Peperstraat 10 ☎ 020/627 0280. Wed–Sun
6–10pm. MAP PP.82-83, POCKET MAP F4

This attractive trattoria
occupies smart canal-side
premises and serves excellent
Italian food – especially the
ravioli. Mains around €20.

Bars

BROUWERIJ 'T IJ

De Gooyer Windmill, Funenkade 7. A 10min
walk east of the Maritime Museum along
Hoogte Kadijk. Daily 3–8pm. MAP PP.82-83,
POCKET MAP H5

Cosy bar and mini-brewery
adjacent to the De Gooyer
windmill. Serves an excellent
range of brews, including the
thunderously strong Columbus.

DE DRUIF

Rapenburgerplein 83. Daily 3pm–1am, Fri &
Sat until 2am. MAP PP.82-83, POCKET MAP G4

Possibly the city's oldest bar,
and certainly one of its more
beguiling, this neighbourhood
joint pulls in an easy-going
crowd.

DE SLUYSWACHT

Jodenbreestraat 1. Daily noon–1am, Fri & Sat until 3am, Sun 11.30am–7pm. MAP PP.82–83, POCKET MAP E4

This pleasant little bar occupies an old and now solitary gabled house that stands sentry by the lock gates opposite the Rembrandthuis. A smashing spot to nurse a beer on a warm summer's night, gazing down the canal towards the Montelbaanstoren.

KHL KOFFIEHUIS

Oostelijke Handelskade 44 ☎ 020/779 1575, ⓦ www.khl.nl. Tues–Thurs 11am–1am, Fri 11am–2am, Sat noon–3am, Sun noon–1am. MAP PP.82–83, POCKET MAP H3

Old-fashioned coffeehouse (not to be confused with coffeeshop) with wooden panelling and heavy red curtains, located in a 1917 state monument. Small but varied menu and live music in the backroom on Saturday and Sunday.

Clubs and music venues

BIMHUIS

Piet Heinkade 3 ☎ 020/788 2188, ⓦ www .bimhuis.nl. MAP PP.82–83, POCKET MAP G2

The city's premier jazz and improvised music venue is located right next the Muziekgebouw, beside the River IJ to the east of Centraal Station. The Bimhuis showcases gigs from Dutch and international artists throughout the week, as well as jam sessions and workshops. There's also a bar and restaurant for concert-goers with pleasant views over the river.

MUZIEKGEBOUW

Piet Heinkade 1 ☎ 020/788 2010, ⓦ www .muziekgebouw.nl. MAP PP.82–83, POCKET MAP G2

PANAMA

Located in a modern glass building overlooking the water, the Muziekgebouw showcases everything from classical through to jazz and rock, and has studios, rehearsal space and convention facilities.

PAKHUIS WILHELMINA

Veemkade 576 ☎ 020/419 3368, ⓦ www. cafépakhuiswilhelmina.nl. MAP PP.82–83, POCKET MAP H3

Tucked away in an old warehouse, this underground venue hosts everything from jazz to pop, funk, punk and folk, with live gigs and DJs from Thursday to Sunday.

PANAMA

Oostelijke Handelskade 4 ☎ 020/311 8689, ⓦ www.panama.nl. MAP PP.82–83, POCKET MAP H3

All-in-one restaurant, bar and nightclub located in the former power plant located right on the river IJ. Many live performances as well as internationally renowned DJs on weekends. One of the coolest spots in the city, *Panama* has played a leading role in spicing up the Eastern docks.

The Museum Quarter and the Vondelpark

During the nineteenth century, Amsterdam grew beyond its restraining canals, gobbling up the surrounding countryside with a slew of new, mostly residential suburbs. Museumplein served as an introduction to these new developments, a large triangular open space surrounded by the cream of the city's museums. The largest is the Rijksmuseum, which occupies a huge late nineteenth-century edifice overlooking the Singelgracht and possesses an exceptional collection of art and applied art. Close by, the more modern Van Gogh Museum boasts the finest assortment of Van Gogh paintings in the world, while the adjacent Stedelijk Museum boasts an outstanding collection of modern art, though it's closed for extensive refurbishment until at least 2012. Out on this side of the city also is the Vondelpark, Amsterdam's largest and most attractive green space, whose gently landscaped rectangle of lawns and paths, lakes and streams provides the perfect place for a lazy picnic between museums. The leafy streets around the park, such as PC Hooftstraat, also provide some of the most upmarket shopping in Amsterdam.

MUSEUMPLEIN

MAP P.96, POCKET MAP C7

Extending south from Stadhouderskade to Van Baerlestraat, **Museumplein**'s wide lawns and gravelled spaces are used for a variety of outdoor activities, from visiting circuses to political demonstrations. There's a **war memorial** here too – it's the group of slim steel blocks about three-quarters of the way down the Museumplein on the left-hand side. It commemorates the women of the wartime concentration camps, particularly those who died at Ravensbruck.

WAR MEMORIAL, MUSEUMPLEIN

THE RIJKSMUSEUM

THE RIJKSMUSEUM

Entrance to the Philips Wing of the Rijksmuseum is on Jan Luijkenstraat
☎ 020/674 7000, ⊕ www.rijksmuseum.nl. Daily 9am–6pm. €12.50. MAP P.96, POCKET MAP C6

The **Rijksmuseum** is without question the country's foremost museum, with one of the world's most comprehensive collections of seventeenth-century Dutch paintings, including twenty or so of **Rembrandt**'s works, plus a healthy sample of canvases by Steen, Hals, Vermeer and their leading contemporaries. The museum also owns an extravagant collection of paintings from every other pre-twentieth-century period of Dutch art and has a vast hoard of applied art and sculpture. The bad news is that there's a major renovation going on at the moment and most of the museum is closed, probably until 2013. The exception is the Rijksmuseum's Philips Wing, whose smallish but eclectic "Masterpieces" exhibition, scheduled to last until the rest of the museum is reopened, is devoted to the paintings of Amsterdam's Golden Age. Bear in mind,

though, that queues can be long, especially in summer and at weekends, so try to book online ahead of time.

Even if you do have to queue, it's still worth the wait, as the selection on display is superb. There are paintings by Rembrandt's pupils – Ferdinand Bol, Gerard Dou and Gabriel Metsu; several wonderful canvases by Frans Hals, such as his scatological *Merry Drinker*; the cool interiors of Vermeer, Gerard ter Borch and Pieter de Hooch; soft, tonal river scenes by the Haarlem artist Salomon van Ruysdael and by Albert Cuyp; the cool church interiors of Pieter Saenredam; and the popular carousing peasants of Jan Steen. However, it's the Rembrandts that steal the show, especially *The Night Watch* of 1642 – perhaps the most famous and probably the most valuable of all the artist's pictures – plus other key works, like a late *Self-Portrait*, a touching depiction of his cowled son, *Titus*, the arresting *Staalmeesters* and *The Jewish Bride*, one of his very last pictures, finished in 1667.

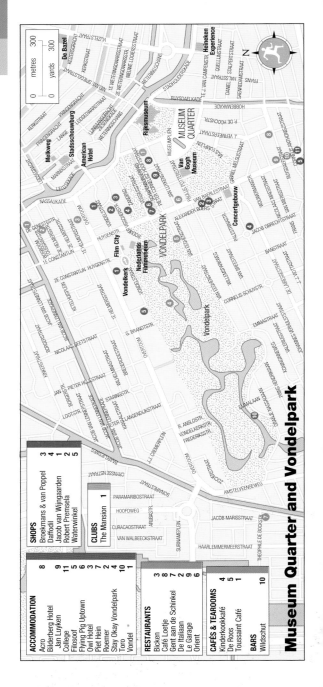

Museum Quarter and Vondelpark

ACCOMMODATION	
Acro	8
Bilderberg Hotel	9
Jan Luyken	11
College	5
Filosoof	6
Flying Pig Uptown	3
Owl Hotel	7
Piet Hein	2
Roemer	4
Stay Okay Vondelpark	10
Toro	
Vondel	1

RESTAURANTS	
Bicken	3
Café Loetje	8
Gent aan de Schinkel	7
De Italiaan	2
Le Garage	9
Orient	6

CAFÉS & TEAROOMS	
Kinderkookkafé	4
De Roos	5
Toussaint Café	1

BARS	
Wildschut	10

SHOPS	
Broekmans & van Poppel	3
Daffodil	4
Jacob van Wijngaarden	1
Robert Premsela	2
Waterwinkel	5

CLUBS	
The Mansion	1

THE VAN GOGH MUSEUM

Paulus Potterstraat 7 ☎ 020/570 5200,
🌐 www.vangoghmuseum.nl. Daily 10am–6pm,
Fri until 10pm. €14, under 17 free. MAP P.96,
POCKET MAP B7

The **Van Gogh Museum**, comprising a fabulous collection of the artist's (1853–90) work, is one of Amsterdam's top attractions. The museum occupies two modern buildings, with the kernel of the collection housed in an angular building at the front designed by a leading light of the De Stijl movement, Gerrit Rietveld, and opened to the public in 1973. Beautifully presented, this part of the museum provides an introduction to the man and his art based on paintings that were mostly inherited from Vincent's art-dealer brother Theo.

All of Van Gogh's key paintings are featured on the **first floor**, displayed chronologically, starting with the dark, sombre works of the early years like *The Potato Eaters* and finishing up with the asylum years at St Rémy and the final, tortured paintings done at Auvers, where Van Gogh lodged for the last three months of his life. It was at Auvers that he painted the frantic *Ears of Wheat* and *Wheatfield with a Reaper*, and

it was a few weeks after completing these last paintings that Van Gogh shot and fatally wounded himself.

The two floors above provide back-up to the main collection. The **second floor** has a study area with access to a detailed computerized account of Van Gogh's life and times, while the third floor has a number of his sketches and a handful of less familiar paintings. The **third floor** also affords space to relevant temporary exhibitions illustrating Van Gogh's artistic influences, or his own influence on other artists, many of whom influenced his work – among them Gauguin and Millet.

To the rear of Rietveld's building, and connected by a ground floor-level escalator, is the ultra-modern curved annexe, completed in 1998. Financed by a Japanese insurance company – the same conglomerate that paid $35 million for one of Van Gogh's *Sunflowers* canvases in 1987 – this provides temporary exhibition space. Most of these exhibitions focus on one aspect or another of Van Gogh's art and draw heavily on the permanent collection, which means that the paintings displayed in the older building are regularly rotated.

VAN GOGH'S THE YELLOW HOUSE

THE CONCERTGEBOUW

Concertgebouwplein 10 ☎ 020/671 8345, ⓦ www.concertgebouw.nl. Tours Sun 12.15pm & Mon 5pm. €10. MAP P.96, POCKET MAP B7

The **Concertgebouw** (Concert Hall) is the home of the famed – and much recorded – Koninklijk (Royal) Concertgebouw Orchestra. When the German composer Brahms visited Amsterdam in the 1870s he was scathing about the locals' lack of culture and in particular their lack of an even halfway suitable venue for his music. In the face of such ridicule, a consortium of Amsterdam businessmen got together to fund the construction of a brand-new concert hall and the result was the Concertgebouw, completed in 1888. Since then it has become renowned among musicians and concertgoers for its marvellous acoustics, and after a facelift and the replacement of its crumbling foundations in the early 1990s it is looking and sounding better than ever. The acoustics of the Grote Zaal (Large Hall) are unparalleled, and the smaller Kleine Zaal regularly hosts chamber concerts. Prices are very reasonable at €30–50, there are free Wednesday lunchtime concerts from September to May, and in July and August they put on a heavily subsidized series of summer concerts.

Tours last a little over an hour and take in the Grote Zaal, the Kleine Zaal, and the various backroom activities behind all this – control rooms, piano stores, dressing rooms and the like.

THE VONDELPARK

MAP P.96, POCKET MAP A7

Amsterdam is short of green spaces, which makes the leafy expanses of the **Vondelpark**, a short stretch from Museumplein and the Concertgebouw, doubly welcome. This is easily the largest and most popular of the city's parks, its network of footpaths used by a healthy slice of the city's back population. The park dates back to 1864, when a group of leading Amsterdammers clubbed together to transform the soggy marshland that lay beyond the Leidsepoort into a landscaped park. The park possesses over 100 species of tree, a wide variety of local and imported plants, and – among many

NEDERLANDS FILMMUSEUM

incidental features – a bandstand, an excellent rose garden, and a network of ponds and narrow waterways that are home to many sorts of wildfowl. There are other animals too: cows, sheep, hundreds of squirrels, plus a large colony of bright-green (and very noisy) parakeets. During the summer the park regularly hosts free concerts and theatrical performances, mostly in its own specially designed open-air theatre.

The park is named after Amsterdam's foremost poet, **Joost van den Vondel** (1587–1679), who ran a hosiery business here in the city, in between writing and hobnobbing with the local elite. Vondel was a kind of Dutch Shakespeare and his *Gijsbrecht van Amstel*, in which he celebrates Dutch life during the Golden Age is one of the classics of Dutch literature. There's a large and somewhat grandiose statue of the man on a plinth near the main entrance to the park.

THE NEDERLANDS FILMMUSEUM AND LIBRARY

Vondelpark 3 ☎ 020/589 1400, ⓦ www .filmmuseum.nl. MAP P.96, POCKET MAP A6

Housed in a fetching nineteenth-century building near the northeastern corner of the Vondelpark, the **Nederlands Filmmuseum** is really more an arthouse cinema (with two screens) than a museum – a showcase for films of all kinds, most of which are shown in their original language, with subtitles in Dutch or sometimes English. There are several screenings nightly, plus regular matinees, and the programme often follows a prescribed theme or subject. Look out also for news of the free screenings of classic movies in the summer. Behind the museum, just outside the park at Vondelstraat 69, the museum's **film library** (Mon, Tues, Thurs & Fri 1–5pm) has a substantial collection of books, magazines and journals, some in English, though they are for reference only.

Shops

BROEKMANS & VAN POPPEL

Van Baerlestraat 92–94. Mon 10am–6pm,
Tues–Fri 9am–6pm, Sat 9am–5pm. MAP P.96,
POCKET MAP B7

Experts in classical music and
opera CDs and sheet music,
this shop has perhaps the best
selection in the city.

DAFFODIL

Jacob Obrechtstraat 41. Tues–Fri noon–6pm,
Sat noon–5pm. MAP P.96, POCKET MAP B8

Behind the Concertgebouw,
this fashionable and very
popular clothes shop features
secondhand designer labels,
mostly from the 1980s
onwards.

JACOB VAN WIJNGAARDEN

Overtoom 135. Mon 1–6pm, Tues–Fri
10am–6pm, Thurs until 9pm, Sat 10am–5pm.
MAP P.96, POCKET MAP A6

The city's best travel bookshop,
with knowledgeable staff and a
huge selection of books, maps,
inflatable and illuminated
globes and more.

ROBERT PREMSELA

Van Baerlestraat 78. Mon noon–6pm, Tues–
Fri 10am–6pm, Sat 10am–5.30pm, Sun
11am–5pm. MAP P.96, POCKET MAP B7

Great art and architecture book
specialist, with plenty of stuff
available in English.

WATERWINKEL

Roelof Hartstraat 10. Mon–Fri 10am–6pm,
Sat 10am–5pm. MAP P.96, POCKET MAP B8

The only thing on offer here
is water – over a hundred
different types of bottled
mineral water from all over
the world. If you're feeling
dehydrated –and flush – try a
bottle of the deluxe Bling H20
studded in Swarovski crystals;
at €49 a pop, it's the haute
couture of spring water.

JACOB VAN WIJNGAARDEN

Cafés and tearooms

KINDERKOOKKAFÉ

Vondelpark 6b (Overtoom 325) ☎ 020/625
3257. Daily 10am–5pm. MAP P.96, POCKET MAP A7

A café run entirely by children
aged 5–12, who cook, waiter
and wash dishes. The food is
simple – pizzas, sandwiches,
cakes – and makes for a very
rewarding experience.

DE ROOS

PC Hooftstraat 183. Mon–Fri 8.30am–9pm,
Sat & Sun until 5.30pm. MAP P.96, POCKET MAP B7

The downstairs café at this New
Age centre on the edge of the
Vondelpark is one of the most
peaceful spots in the city,
selling a range of drinks and
organic snacks and meals.
There's also an upstairs
bookshop, and any number of
courses in yoga and meditation.

TOUSSAINT CAFÉ

Bosboom Toussaintstraat 26. Daily
10am–11pm, Fri & Sat until 1am. MAP P.96,
POCKET MAP B5

This cosy, very friendly café not
far from the Vondelpark makes
a nice spot for lunch – excellent
sandwiches, toasties, *uitsmijters*

as well as a tapas-type menu, although service can be slow.

Restaurants

BICKEN

Overtoom 28 ☎ 020/689 3999. Daily 5.30–10.30pm. MAP P.96, POCKET MAP B6

Trendy and minimalistic restaurant offering fresh, seasonal products with an international twist. Creative mains will set you back around €25.

CAFÉ LOETJE

Johannes Vermeerstraat 52 ☎ 020/662 8173. Mon–Fri 11am–midnight, Sat 5.30–11.30pm; closed Sun. MAP P.96, POCKET MAP C8

Excellent steaks, fries and salads are the order of the day here at this *eetcafé*. The service can be patchy, but the food is great, and inexpensive. The pleasant outdoor terrace in the summer is a bonus.

GENT AAN DE SCHINKEL

Theophile de Bockstraat 1 ☎ 020/388 2851. Daily 11.30am–3.30pm & 5.30–10pm. MAP P.96, POCKET MAP A5

Situated just outside the top end of the Vondelpark, across the pedestrian bridge, this is a lovely corner restaurant on a busy canal, serving Belgian and fusion cuisine and a huge range of bottled Belgian beers to enjoy on their summer terrace.

DE ITALIAAN

Bosboom Toussaintstraat 29 ☎ 020/683 6854. Wed–Sun 6–10pm. MAP P.96, POCKET MAP B5

A first-rate range of Italian dishes, both à la carte and in a set menu – three courses for €25. The pizzas are cooked in a wood oven.

LE GARAGE

Ruysdaelstraat 54 ☎ 020/679 7176. Daily 6–11pm, Mon–Fri also noon–2.30pm. MAP P.96, POCKET MAP C8

This elegant restaurant, with an eclectic French and Italian menu, is popular with a media crowd, since it's run by a well-known Dutch TV cook. Call to reserve at least a week in advance and dress to impress. Three-course menus are €45.

ORIENT

Van Baerlestraat 21 ☎ 020/673 4958. Daily 5–10pm. MAP P.96, POCKET MAP B7

Excellently prepared Indonesian dishes, with a wide range to choose from; vegetarians are very well taken care of, and the service is generally good. Expect to pay around €20 for a *rijsttafel*.

Bars

WILDSCHUT

Roelof Hartplein 1. Mon–Fri 8.30am–12.30am, Sat & Sun 10am–12.30am. MAP P.96, POCKET MAP C8

Not far from the Concertgebouw, this bar is famous for its Art Deco trimmings, and its large interior and outside seating in summer. The nicest place to drink in the area, and with a decent menu too.

Clubs

THE MANSION

Hobbemastraat 2 ☎ 020/616 6664. Club Fri & Sat 9pm–3am; bar Mon–Thurs 6.30pm–1am, Fri & Sat 6.30pm–3am; restaurant Mon–Thurs 7–11pm, Fri & Sat 7pm–midnight. MAP P.96, POCKET MAP C6

Brassy and over the top restaurant-cum-club with ostrich leather and gold leaf on the walls. Dress to impress and bring bags of money if you want to be a part of the jet set in-crowd.

The outer districts

Amsterdam is a small city, and the majority of its residential outer districts are easily reached from the city centre. The south holds most of interest, kicking off with the vibrant De Pijp quarter, home to the Heineken Experience and the 1930s architecture of the Nieuw Zuid (New South), which is also near the enjoyable woodland area of the Amsterdamse Bos. As for the other districts, you'll find a good deal less reason to make the effort, although the Tropenmuseum, a short walk from the Muiderpoort gate in Amsterdam East, is worth a special journey, and further south the Amsterdam ArenA, home to Ajax, is a must-see for football fans.

DE PIJP

MAP PP.104–105, POCKET MAP D7

Across Boerenwetering, the canal to the east of the Rijksmuseum and the Museumplein (see p.94), lies the busy heart of the Oud Zuid (Old South) – the district known as **De Pijp** ("The Pipe"), Amsterdam's first real suburb. New development beyond the Singelgracht began around 1870, but after laying down the street plans, the city council left the actual house-building to private developers. They made the most of the arrangement and constructed long rows of cheaply built and largely featureless five- and six-storey buildings, and it is these that still dominate the area today. The district's name comes from the characteristically narrow terraced streets running between long, sombre canyons of brick tenements: the apartments here were said to resemble pipe-drawers, since each had a tiny street frontage but extended deep into the building. De Pijp remains one of the city's more closely knit communities, and is home to a large proportion of new arrivals – Surinamese, Moroccan, Turkish and Asian.

Trams #16 and #24, beginning at Centraal Station, travel along the northern part of De Pijp's main drag, Ferdinand Bolstraat, as far as Albert Cuypstraat.

THE WETERING CIRCUIT

MAP PP.104–105, POCKET MAP D7

At the southern end of Vijzelgracht, on the city-centre side of the Singelgracht, is the **Wetering circuit** roundabout, which has two low-key memorials to World War II. On

HEINEKEN EXPERIENCE

ALBERT CUYPSTRAAT MARKET

the southwestern corner of the roundabout, by the canal, is a sculpture of a wounded man holding a bugle; it was here, on March 12, 1945, that thirty people were shot by the Germans in reprisal for acts of sabotage by the Dutch Resistance – given that the war was all but over, it's hard to imagine a crueller or more futile action. Across the main street, the second memorial in the form of a brick wall commemorates H.M. van Randwijk, a Resistance leader.

THE HEINEKEN EXPERIENCE

Stadhouderskade 78. Tram #16, #24 from Centraal station ☎ 020/523 9666. ◎ www .heinekenexperience.com. Daily 11am–7pm. €15. MAP PP.104–105, POCKET MAP B7

On the northern edge of De Pijp, just beyond the Wetering Circuit, the former **Heineken brewery**, a whopping modern building beside the Singelgracht canal, now holds the **Heineken Experience**. The brewery was Heineken's headquarters from 1864 to 1988, when the company was restructured and brewing was moved to a location out of town. Since then, Heineken has developed the site as a

tourist attraction with lots of gimmicky but fun attractions such as virtual reality tours and displays on the history of Heineken, from advertising campaigns to beer-making. The old brewing facilities with their vast copper vats are included on the tour, but for many the main draw is the free beer you get to quaff at the end in the bar.

ALBERT CUYPSTRAAT MARKET

MAP PP.104–105, POCKET MAP D8–E7

Ferdinand Bolstraat, running north–south, is De Pijp's main street, but the long east–west thoroughfare of Albert Cuypstraat is its heart. The general **market** here (daily except Sun 10am–5pm) – which stretches for over a kilometre between Ferdinand Bolstraat and Van Woustraat – is the largest in the city, with a huge array of stalls selling everything from carrots and raw-herring sandwiches to saucepans and Day Glo thongs. Check out the ethnic shops that flank the market on each side, and the good-value Indian and Surinamese restaurants down the side streets.

THE SARPHATIPARK

Tram #3 & 25. MAP PP.104–105, POCKET MAP E8

Leafy **Sarphatipark** provides a welcome splash of greenery among the surrounding brick and concrete. The park, complete with footpaths and a sinewy lake, was laid out before the construction of De Pijp got underway, and was initially intended as a place for the bourgeoisie to take a picnic.

THE NIEUW ZUID

MAP PP.104–105, POCKET MAP B9

Southwest of De Pijp, the **Nieuw Zuid** (New South) was the first properly planned extension to the city since the concentric canals of the seventeenth century. The Dutch architect Hendrik Petrus Berlage was responsible for the overall plan, but much of the implementation passed to a pair of prominent architects of the Amsterdam School, Michael de Klerk and Piet Kramer, and it's the playful vision of these two – turrets and bulging windows, sloping roofs and frilly balustrades – that you see in some of the buildings of the Nieuw Zuid today. These architectural peccadilloes have helped make the Nieuw Zuid one of Amsterdam's most sought-after addresses. The best example of the area's style is the housing estate located just north of the Amstel canal, **De Dageraad** (see opposite). Apollolaan and, a little way to the east, Churchilllaan, are especially favoured and home to some of the city's most attractive properties. Locals pop to the shops on Beethovenstraat, the main drag running south right through the district, and stroll

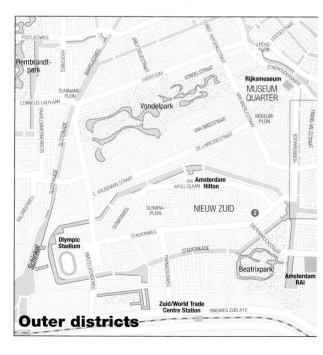

Outer districts

through the languid greenery of the Beatrixpark, or, slightly further out, the Amsterdamse Bos, but there's not much to attract the visitor who isn't a student of modern architecture.

THE AMSTERDAM HILTON

Apollolaan 138. MAP PP.104–105, POCKET MAP A9

One historic footnote that might entice you this far south is the **Amsterdam Hilton**, where John Lennon and Yoko Ono staged their famous week-long "Bed-In" for peace in 1969. More recently the *Hilton* was the centre of Dutch media attention when Herman Brood – a Dutch singer, painter and professional junkie – committed suicide by jumping from the roof.

DE DAGERAAD

Tram #4 runs along Van Woustraat; get off at Jozef Israelskade and it's a 5min walk to De Dageraad. MAP PP.104–105, POCKET MAP E9

Built between 1919 and 1922, the **De Dageraad** housing project was – indeed, is – public housing inspired by socialist utopianism, a grand vision built to elevate the working class, hence its name, "The Dawn". The handsome brick and stone work of the Berlage Lyceum marks the start of De Dageraad, with 350 workers' houses stretching beyond to either side of Pieter Lodewijk Takstraat and Burgemeester Tellegenstraat. The architects used a reinforced concrete frame as an underlay to each house, thus permitting folds, tucks and curves in the brick exteriors. Strong, angular doors, sloping roofs and turrets punctuate the facades, and you'll find a corner tower at the end of every block – it's stunning.

CLUBS	
Arena	1

COFFEESHOPS	
Greenhouse	2

RESTAURANTS	
L'Angoletto	1

ACCOMMODATION	
Hotel Arena	1
Xaviera Hollander B&B	2

THE AMSTERDAMSE BOS

Main entrance near the visitor centre at the junction of Amstelveenseweg and Van Nijenrodeweg, 3km south of the west end of the Vondelpark (see p.98). Trams #16 & #24 from Centraal Station and the Heineken Experience (see p.00); it's about 350m from the nearest tram stop to the east end of Bosbaan and the visitor centre.
ⓦ www.amsterdamsebos.nl. MAP PP.104-105, POCKET MAP B9

With ten square kilometres of wooded parkland, the **Amsterdamse Bos** (Amsterdam Forest), to the southwest of the Nieuw Zuid, is the city's largest open space. Planted during the 1930s, the park was a large-scale attempt to provide gainful work for the city's unemployed. Originally a bleak area of flat and marshy fields, it combines a rural feel with that of a well-tended city park – and thus the "forest" tag is something of a misnomer.

In the north of the Bos, the **Bosbaan** is a kilometre-long dead-straight canal, popular for boating and swimming, and there are children's playgrounds and spaces for various sports, including ice skating. There's also a goat farm (mid-March to Oct daily except Tues 10am–5pm, Nov to early March also closed on Mon; ⓣ020/645 5034) and a nature reserve just to the south with bison and sheep. Canoes and pedaloes can be rented west of the Bosbaan at **Grote Vijver** ("big pond"; April–Sept daily 10.30am–7.30pm; ⓣ020/645 7831), or you can simply walk or jog your way around a choice of six clearly marked trails. The **Bezoekerscentrum** (visitor centre; daily noon–5pm; free; ⓣ020/545 6100), at the main entrance to the Bos at Bosbaanweg 5,

De Pijp

Singelgracht
STADHOUDERSKADE

1E JACOB VAN CAMPENSTRAAT
HOBBEMAKADE
Boerenwetering
QUELLIJNSTRAAT
BOLSTRAAT
1E VAN DER HELSTSTR
Heineken Experience

DANIEL STALPERTSTRAAT
RUYSDAELKADE
SAENREDAMSTR.
FRANS HALSSTRAAT
GERARD DOUSTRAAT
ALBERT CUYPSTRAAT
GOVERT FLINCKSTRAAT
1E JAN STEENSTRAAT
1E JAN VAN DER HEIJDENSTRAAT

DE PIJP
SWEELINCKSTRAAT
Sarphatipark
SARPHATIPARK

N

CEINTUURBAAN
VAN OSTADESTRAAT
RUSTENBURGERSTRAAT
FERDINAND BOLSTRAAT
KAREL DU JARDINSTRAAT
2E VAN DER HELSTSTRAAT
KAREL DU JARDINSTRAAT
LUTMASTRAAT
MESSAUSSTRAAT
W. PASSTOORSTRAAT
LUTMASTRAAT

OUD ZUID

De Dageraad

JOZEF ISRAELSKADE

BARS	
Café Krull	14
Chocolate Bar	10
De Groene Vlinder	6
Pilsvogel	5
Wynbar Boelen&Boelen	3

SHOPS	
Beadazzled	2
Blond	1

ACCOMMODATION	
Hotel Okura	2
Van Ostade	1

RESTAURANTS	
Bazar	7
De Duvel	12
Hotel Okura	15
De Ondeugd	2
Saray	8
Trez	4
De Waaghals	1
Zagros	13

CAFÉS & TEAROOMS	
Granny	11
Vishandel De Zeemeermin	9

0	metres	200
0	yards	200

CAFÉ IN THE AMSTERDAMSE BOS PARK

provides maps and information. There's also a pancake house, *Boerderij Meerzicht*, at the east of the Bosbaan at Koenenkade 56 (late Feb to Oct Tues–Sun 10am–7pm; Nov to mid-Feb Fri–Sun 10am–6pm; ☎ 020/679 2744) and bike rental close by (April–Oct daily 10am–6pm; ☎ 020/644 5473) – cycling being the best way of getting around.

COBRA MUSEUM

Sandbergplein 1, Amstelveen. Bus #170, #171 and #172, stop 'busstation Amstelveen' in front of the museum. ☎ 020/547 5050, ⓦ www.cobra-museum.nl. Tues–Sun 11am–5pm. €9.50. MAP PP.184–105. POCKET MAP B9

The **CoBrA Museum of Modern Art**, located well to the south of the Amsterdamse Bos entrance, close to the Amstelveen bus station, is soothingly white. Its glass walls give a view of the canal behind, displaying the works of the artists of the CoBrA movement, which was founded in 1948. The movement grew out of artistic developments in

the cities of Copenhagen, Brussels and Amsterdam – hence the name. CoBrA's first exhibition, held at Amsterdam's Stedelijk Museum, showcased the big, colourful canvases, with bold lines and confident forms, for which the movement became famous. Their work displayed a spontaneity and inclusivity that was unusual for the art world of the time and it stirred a veritable hornet's next of artistic controversy. You'll only find a scattering of their work here in the gallery, but there's enough to get an idea of what CoBrA were about, not least in **Karel Appel**'s weird bird sculpture outside, and the brash, childlike paintings of Appel inside – in many ways Appel was the movement's leading light. Upstairs, the museum hosts regular temporary exhibitions of works by contemporary artists. There's a good shop, too, with plenty of prints and books on the movement, plus a bright café where you can gaze upon Appel's sculpture at length.

THE MUIDERPOORT

Plantage Middenlaan. MAP PP.184–185, POCKET MAP H6

Amsterdam East begins with Amsterdam's old eastern gate, the **Muiderpoort**, a Neoclassical affair complete with a flashy cupola and grandiosely carved pediment. Napoleon staged a triumphal entry into the city through here in 1811, but his imperial pleasure was tempered by his half-starved troops, who could barely be restrained from helping themselves in a city of (what was to them) amazing luxury.

THE TROPENMUSEUM

Linnaeusstraat 2. Tram #9 from Centraal station. ☎ 020/568 8200, ⓦ www .tropenmuseum.nl. Daily 10am–5pm. €9; 6- to 17-year-olds €5. MAP PP.184–185, POCKET MAP H6

Despite its general lack of appeal, the East district does have one obvious attraction – the **Tropenmuseum**, perched on the corner of another of the city's municipal green spaces, the Oosterpark. With its cavernous central hall and three floors of gallery space, this museum has room to focus on themes such as the world's cultural and historical influences, and impresses with its applied art.

The first floor is dedicated to Dutch colonialism, focusing on Indonesia and the Pacific. Among the artefacts, there are Javanese stone friezes, elaborate carved wooden boats from New Guinea and, perhaps strangest of all, ritual ancestor "Bis poles" cut from giant New Guinea mangroves. The collection is imaginatively presented and there are also creative and engaging displays devoted to such subjects as music-making and puppetry. In addition there are intriguing reconstructions, down to sounds and smells, of typical settings from different countries, such as a Jamaican café or a Surinamese logger's hut.

While you're here, be sure to try the inexpensive **restaurant**, the *Ekeko*, which serves tropical snacks and lunches, including popular national dishes from featured countries.

AMSTERDAM ARENA

Arena Boulevard 1. Metro to Strandvliet or ArenA ☎ 020/311 1336, ⓦ www .amsterdamarena.nl. April–Sept daily 9am–6pm; Oct–March Mon–Sat & last Sun of the month 9am–5pm. Museum and stadium tour €10.50, museum only €3.50. MAP PP.184–185, POCKET MAP F9

It's well worth the fifteen-minute metro ride to visit the **Ajax Museum** and take a tour of the stadium at the same time. The museum pays homage to Johan Marco Cruyff and van Basten and displays paraphernalia from the club's European campaigns. The main draw, however, is an hour-long, behind-the-scenes tour.

Shops

BEADAZZLED

Sarphatipark 6. Mon 1–6pm, Tues–Fri
10.30am–6pm, Sat 10.30am–5pm.
MAP PP.104–105, POCKET MAP D8

Beads in all shapes and colours
as well as bags, cheerfully
decorated lamps and other
accessories, bound to make
most women greedy.

BLOND

Gerard Doustraat 69. Mon noon–6pm, Tues–
Fri 10am–6pm, Sat 10am–5pm. MAP PP.104–105,
POCKET MAP D7

Popular gift shop with
hand-painted and personalized
pottery, bed linen, towels and
note blocks, mainly in the
colour pink.

Coffeeshops

GREENHOUSE

Tolstraat 91. Tram #4. Daily 9am–1am, Fri &
Sat until 2am. MAP PP.104–105, POCKET MAP F8

Consistently sweeps the boards
at the annual Cannabis Cup,
with medals for its dope as
well as "Best Coffeeshop" –
these guys are extremely
knowledgeable in their

"grassy" field. Tolstraat is
down to the south, but worth
the trek: if you're only buying
once, buy here. Also a branch
nearer to the centre at O.Z.
Voorburgwal 191.

Cafés and tearooms

GRANNY

1e van der Helststraat 45. Tues–Sat
9am–6pm. MAP PP.104–105, POCKET MAP D8

Just off the Albert Cuypstraat
market, adorned with
low-hanging beaded
lamp-shades and faded photos
of canal scenes, this place is
known for its terrific
appelgebak, had with whipped
cream for that full-on homely
experience.

VISHANDEL DE ZEEMEERMIN

Albert Cuypstraat 93. Mon–Sat 9am–5pm.
MAP PP.104–105, POCKET MAP D8

What better way to round off
your visit to the market than to
sample the delights of this
excellent – and typical – Dutch
fish stall. If you're not brave
enough for the raw herring
there are cooked offerings too,
such as calamari.

Restaurants

BAZAR

Albert Cuypstraat 182 ☎ 020/675 0544. Mon–
Thurs 5–11pm, Fri 5pm–midnight, Sat
4.30pm–midnight, Sun 4.30–11pm. MAP
PP.104–105, POCKET MAP D7

This cavernous converted
church is usually buzzing with
activity long after the market
traders have packed up. A lively
place to eat dinner; choose
from the Middle Eastern and
North African influenced menu
with tasty *mezze* and kebab.

DE DUVEL

DE DUVEL

1e van der Helststraat 59 ☎ 020/675 7517.
Daily 11am–4pm & 6–11pm, no lunch on Mon.
MAP PP.104–105, POCKET MAP O8

Immensely popular *eetcafé*,
always crowded, so be sure to
book ahead. Mains like duck
breast, *saté* and huge salads
for around €16. Also a
popular drinking spot after
dinner.

HOTEL OKURA

Ferdinand Bolstraat 333 ☎ 020/678 7111.
Daily from 6.30pm. MAP PP.104–105,
POCKET MAP D9

This five-star hotel has two
Michelin-starred restaurants –
the sushi restaurant *Yamazato*,
with over fifty specialities, and
the *French Ciel Bleu* situated
on the 23rd floor, offering
amazing views of the city –
plus the renowned grill-plate
restaurant *Teppanyaki
Sazanka*, which makes it one

TEPPANYAKI SAZANKA AT THE HOTEL OKURA

of the finest places to dine in
the city. Reckon on at least
€50 per person. Advance
bookings essential.

L'ANGOLETTO

Hemonystraat 18 ☎ 020/676 4182. Daily
except Sat 6–10.30pm. MAP PP.104–105,
POCKET MAP E7

Just about everyone's favourite
Italian, inexpensive and always
packed, with long wooden
tables and benches that create a
very sociable atmosphere. Not
everything they serve is shown
on the menu, so keep an eye on
the glass showcase in front of
the kitchen for any specials. No
bookings, so just turn up and
hope for the best.

DE ONDEUGD

Ferdinand Bolstraat 13 ☎ 020/672 0651.
Mon–Sat 6–11pm. MAP PP.104–105,
POCKET MAP D7

A long time local favourite,
presenting a French-oriented
menu with the occasional
Eastern twist. Prices are
reasonable, with a decent
boeuf bourguignon or
dorade with lemon puree at
around €18.

SARAY

Gerard Doustraat 33 ☎ 020/671 9216. Tues–
Sun 5–11pm. MAP PP.104–105, POCKET MAP D8

Excellent Turkish eatery down
in the De Pijp neighbourhood.
Its dark-wood, candle lit
interior and living room
ambience bestow an inviting
backdrop for a leisurely dinner.
It's cheap too, with main
courses from €12 and mixed
mezze €7 per person.

TREZ

Saenredamstraat 39 ☎ 020/676 2495. Tues–
Sun 6–10.30pm. MAP PP.104–105, POCKET MAP D7

Intimate little place, with good
views of the chef cooking
Mediterranean-inspired dishes
in the open kitchen. Limited

menu but very reasonably priced, with nothing exceeding €20. Three-course menu €27.50.

DE WAAGHALS

Frans Halsstraat 29 ☏ 020/679 9609. Tues–Sun 5–9.30pm. MAP PP.104–105, POCKET MAP D7

Well-prepared organic dishes in this cooperative-run restaurant near the Albert Cuyp. This place gets busy early so book ahead to be sure of a table. The menu changes twice a month, and though the food takes a while to prepare, the rewards are delicious and generously portioned. Mains around €15. No credit cards.

ZAGROS

Albert Cuypstraat 50 ☏ 020/670 0461. Tues–Sun 5–10.30pm. MAP PP.104–105, POCKET MAP C8

Popular no-frills Kurdish restaurant run by four brothers. Serves inexpensive traditional dishes from around €3.50 for starters and €13 for marinated lamb and chicken mains. Fish and vegetarian options available too.

Bars

CAFÉ KRULL

Sarphatipark 2. Daily 10.30am–1am, Fri & Sat until 2am. MAP PP.104–105, POCKET MAP D8

On the corner of 1e van der Helststraat, a few metres from the Albert Cuyp, this is an atmospheric and lively place. Drinks and snacks all day long.

CHOCOLATE BAR

1e van der Helststraat 62a. Mon–Thurs 10am–1am, Fri & Sat 10am–3am, Sun 11am–1am. MAP PP.104–105, POCKET MAP D8

Cool, disco-inspired café-bar that's open for tasty food or cocktails any time of the day. Perch at the bar on leather stools or lounge in the cosy room out the back. It's a shame

that service can be somewhat patchy.

DE GROENE VLINDER

Albert Cuypstraat 130. Daily 10am–1am, Fri & Sat until 3am. MAP PP.104–105, POCKET MAP D8

Great views on the bustling market from this split-level café with cheap daily specials and bulky salads.

PILSVOGEL

Gerard Douplein 14 ☏ 020/664 6483. Daily 10am–1am, Fri & Sat until 3am. MAP PP.104–105, POCKET MAP D7

Favourite drinking spot for style-conscious 30-somethings, enjoying the laidback atmosphere and decent tapas as well as the good selection of Spanish wines.

WYNBAR BOELEN&BOELEN

1e van der Helststraat 50. Tues–Thurs & Sun 6pm–midnight, Fri & Sat 6pm–1am. MAP PP.104–105, POCKET MAP D7

Tasteful wine bar close to Albert Cuypstraat market with a huge selection of wines. A heated terrace provides alfresco eating even in the cooler months, and the French-inspired menu offers seafood delights such as a half-dozen oysters for €14.

Clubs

ARENA

's-Gravensandestraat 51. Metro to Weesperplein, then an 8min walk ☏ 020/850 2400. ⓦ www.hotelarena.nl. Fri & Sat 10/11pm–4am. MAP PP.104–105, POCKET MAP H6

Hip club set in a restored chapel adjoining a hotel that used to be an orphanage and an asylum. Open Fridays and Saturdays, with occasional Salsa nights and special parties hosted on a Sunday. International DJs sometimes drop by – and that's when you can expect the entrance fee to jump from around €13 to €20.

Day-trips from Amsterdam

Amsterdammers may well tell you that there's nothing remotely worth seeing outside their own city, but the fact is you're spoilt for choice, with fast and efficient rail connections putting about a third of the country within easy reach on a day-trip. There are any number of places you can reach, including most of the towns of the Randstaad conurbation that stretches south and east of Amsterdam and encompasses the country's other big cities, The Hague, Utrecht and Rotterdam, but we've picked a few of the closest highlights. The easiest trip you could make is to Haarlem, just fifteen minutes away by train, a pleasant provincial town that is home to the outstanding Frans Hals Museum. There's also the showcase of the country's flower growers, the Keukenhof Gardens, worth visiting in spring and summer, while to the north of Amsterdam the most obvious targets are the old seaports bordering the freshwater IJsselmeer and Markermeer lakes, formerly – before the enclosing dykes were put in – the choppy and unpredictable saltwater Zuider Zee. No trains venture out along this coast, but it's an easy bus ride from Amsterdam, as well as to the beguiling one-time shipbuilding centre of Edam. Edam is, of course, famous for its cheese, but its open-air cheese market is not a patch on that of Alkmaar, an amiable small town forty minutes by train northwest from Amsterdam.

HAARLEM

HAARLEM

An easy fifteen-minute train journey (6 hourly) from Amsterdam's Centraal Station, **Haarlem** has a very different feel from its big-city neighbour. Once a flourishing cloth-making centre, the town avoided the worst excesses of industrialization and nowadays it's an easily absorbed place with an attractive centre studded with fine old buildings. The **Grote Kerk** (Mon–Sat 10am–4pm; €2), right in the centre of town on the Grote Markt, is well worth seeing, a soaring Gothic church with a magnificent eighteenth-century organ. But the real draw is the outstanding **Frans Hals Museum**, located in the Oudemannhuis or almshouse where the artist spent his last and, for some, his most brilliant years. Located at Groot Heiligland 62 (Tues–Sat 11am–5pm, Sun noon–5pm; €10; ☎023/511 57 75, ⓦ www .franshalsmuseum.nl), the museum is a five-minute stroll south from the Grote Markt – take pedestrianized Warmoesstraat and then Schagchelstraat and keep straight ahead.

The museum has a number of works by Haarlem painters other than Hals, with canvases by Jan van Scorel, Karel van Mander and Cornelis Cornelisz van Haarlem. Chief among the paintings by Hals is the set of "Civic Guard" portraits with which he made his name. Displayed together, these make a powerful impression, alongside the artist's later, darker works, the most notable of which are the twin Regents and Regentesses of the Oudemannenhuis itself.

THE KEUKENHOF GARDENS

Stationsweg 166, Lisse ☎ 025/2465 555, ⓦ www.keukenhof.com. Late March to late May daily 8am–7.30pm. €14.

The pancake-flat fields extending south from Haarlem towards Leiden are the heart of the **Dutch bulbfields**, whose bulbs and blooms support a billion-dollar industry and some ten-thousand growers, as well as attracting tourists in droves. The small town of **Lisse**, halfway between Leiden and Haarlem, is home to the **Keukenhof Gardens**, the largest flower gardens in the world. Its name literally meaning "kitchen garden", the site is the former estate of a fifteenth-century countess, who used to grow herbs and vegetables for her dining table. Some seven million flowers are on show for their full flowering period, complemented, in case of especially harsh winters, by 5000 square metres of glasshouses holding indoor displays. You could easily spend a whole day here, swooning among the sheer abundance of it all, but to get the best of it you need to come early, before the tour buses pack the place. There are several restaurants in the extensive grounds, and well-marked paths take you all the way through the gardens, which specialize in daffodils, hyacinths and tulips.

To get to the Keukenhof by public transport from Amsterdam, take the train to Leiden (every 20min) and then bus #54 (every 15min; 30min) from the adjacent bus station. You can also purchase a combination ticket (€21) at the tourist offices in Amsterdam, The Hague, Schiphol airport and Haarlem or at the Connexxion sales points, which include bus transport from these locations and the entrance fee to the Keukenhof.

VOLENDAM

The former fishing village of **Volendam** is the largest of the Markermeer towns and was once something of an artists' retreat, visited by Renoir and Picasso in its day and always a favoured location for local painters. The Volendams Museum, on the edge of the town centre at Zeestraat 41 (daily 10am–5pm; €2.50) has lots of local work on display, not least a series of mosaics made up of 11 million cigar bands, the work of a nutty local

THE KEUKENHOF GARDENS

artist, and the comfy downstairs café of the *Hotel Spaander* on the waterfront is crammed full of seaside scenes and portraits contributed in lieu of rent over the years.

Volendam is reachable by bus #110 and #118 from outside Amsterdam Centraal Station; the journey takes half an hour.

MARKEN

Stuck out in the freshwater Markermeer, the tiny island of **Marken** was pretty much a closed community, supported by a small fishing industry, until its road connection to the mainland was completed in 1957. Nowadays, the fishing has all but disappeared, though the island – or rather its one and only village, Marken – retains a picturesque charm of immaculately maintained green wooden houses, clustered on top of artificial mounds first raised to protect the islanders from the sea. There are two main parts to the village: Havenbuurt, around the harbour, where the waterfront is dotted with souvenir shops, often staffed by locals in traditional costume; and the quieter Kerkbuurt, centred on the church, whose narrow lanes are lined by ancient dwellings and one-time eel-smoking houses.

You can take a ferry to Marken from Volendam (March–Oct daily 11am–5pm; every 30–45min; €7 return); the journey takes 25 minutes. The ferries leave you right in the harbour. Or you can get there direct from Centraal Station on bus #111 (every 30min; 35min). The bus drops passengers beside the car park on the edge of Marken village, from where it's a five-minute walk to the centre.

MARKEN HOUSE

EDAM

Considering the international fame of the red balls of cheese that carry its name, you might expect the village of **Edam**, just 12km or so up along the coast from Marken, to be jam-packed with tourists. In fact, Edam usually lacks the crowds of its island neighbour and remains a delightful, good-looking and prosperous little town of neat brick houses and slender canals. Nowadays, the one real crowd puller is Edam's **cheese market**, held every Wednesday morning from July to late August on the Kaasmarkt (10.30am–12.30pm), but the real pleasure is in aimlessly wandering its streets and canals, and maybe renting a bike to cycle down to the water. Bike rental is available at Ronald Schot, Grote Kerkstraat 7 (☎029/937 2155, ⊛www.ronaldschot.nl); a day costs €8.50.

Bus #112 takes 40min to reach Edam from Centraal Station. The bus station is on the southwest edge of town, on Singelweg, a five-minute walk from the main square, Damplein.

ALKMAAR

Forty minutes north of Amsterdam by train, the small town of **Alkmaar** provides a pleasant glimpse of provincial Holland, with an old centre still surrounded by its moat, and a cluster of medieval and Renaissance-era buildings. It has some low-key things to see – the **Biermuseum De Boom** (Mon–Sat 1–4pm; €3.50), above the bar of the same name, has three floors devoted to the art of making and distributing beer, and opposite the town's main St Laurenskerk there's a local museum, the **Stedelijk Museum** (Tues–Sat 10am–5pm, Sun noon–5pm; €3), with paintings, maps and models of Alkmaar during its glory seventeenth-century years.

But the town is best known for its **cheese market** (mid-March to Sept Fri 10am–12.30pm), an ancient affair that these days ranks as one of the most extravagant tourist spectacles in the country. Cheese has been sold on the main square, Waagplein, since the 1300s, and although it's no longer a serious commercial concern, the market continues to draw the crowds. If you want a good view, get here early, as by opening time visitors are already thick on the ground. The ceremony starts with the buyers sniffing, crumbling, and finally tasting each cheese, followed by intensive bartering. Once a deal has been concluded, the cheeses – golden discs of Gouda mainly – are borne away on ornamental carriers for weighing. The porters, who bear the carriers, wear white trousers and shirt plus a black hat whose coloured bands – green, blue, red or yellow – represent the four companies that comprise the cheese porters' guild. Payment for the cheeses, tradition has it, takes place in the cafés around the square.

From Alkmaar's train and bus station, it's a ten-minute walk to the centre of town: keep straight outside the station along Spoorstraat, take the first right down Snaarmanslaan and then left at busy Geesterweg, which leads over the old city moat to St Laurenskerk. From the church, it's another five minutes' walk east along Langestraat to the tourist office, housed in the Waag on Waagplein.

ALKMAAR CHEESES

Restaurants

DIJKERS

Warmoesstraat 5, Haarlem ☎ 023/551 1564.
Daily except Tues–10am–10pm.
Trendy and colourful spot with an inspiring international menu offering everything from Peruvian *ceviche* to Italian saltimbocca for around €18.

DE FORTUNA

Spuistraat 3, Edam ☎ 0299/371 671.
Daily 6–10pm.
This is a first-rate hotel restaurant, with an imaginative, modern menu using local and seasonal ingredients.

HET HOF VAN ALKMAAR

Hof van Sonoy 1, Alkmaar ☎ 072/512 1222.
Mon–Wed 10am–9pm, Thurs 10am–9.30pm,
Fri & Sat 10am–10pm, Sun 11am–9.30pm.
Pretty good for both lunch and dinner, a delightfully restored medieval nunnery that does inexpensive omelettes and sandwiches during the day and tasty Dutch cuisine in the evening, with mains for €15–20.

HOTEL SPAANDER

Haven 35, Volendam ☎ 0299/363 705. Daily noon–9.30pm.
This creaky old hotel right on the waterfront in Volendam is very much the hub of things in the town, with a nice bar for a drink or a coffee and a good brasserie serving lots of fishy specialities for lunch and dinner.

JACOBUS PIECK

Warmoesstraat 18, Haarlem ☎ 023/532 6144.
Mon 11am–4pm, Tues–Sat 11am–4pm & 5.30–10pm.
Welcoming place that's a good bet for both lunch and dinner, with burgers and salads during the day and a Mediterranean-inspired menu in the evening, featuring pasta with mussels and mixed *antipasti*. There's a secluded garden too.

LAND EN ZEEZICHT

Havenbuurt 6, Marken ☎ 0299/601 302. Daily 11am–8.30pm.
More of a lunch than dinner spot, but very cosy, overlooking the harbour and serving a mean smoked-eel sandwich.

LA PLUME

Lange Veerstraat 1, Haarlem ☎ 023/531 3202. Daily 5.30–11pm.
A affordable restaurant with a tasty range of traditional Dutch dishes. Mains €15–20.

RESTAURANT DE BIOS

Gedempte Nieuwesloot 54, Alkmaar ☎ 072/512 4422 Tues & Wed noon–10pm, Thurs–Sat 10am–1am, Sun noon–10pm.
This popular restaurant serves excellent Dutch food with a French slant – mains for around €20.

Bars

CAFÉ STAPPER

Verdronkenoord 127, Alkmaar. Daily 11am–1am.
Very friendly bar with music right in the centre of Alkmaar; next door there's another, equally convivial bar, *De Pilaren*, which has regular live music.

IN DEN UIVER

Riviervischmarkt 13, Haarlem. Mon–Thurs 3pm–2am, Fri & Sat 2pm–4am, Sun 2pm–2am.
Intimate brown café located in a former fish shop, with a wide selection of *jenevers* as well as many wines by the glass. Live music on Thursday and Sunday.

Hotels

Despite a slew of new hotels, from chic designer places through to chain high-rises, hotel accommodation in Amsterdam can still be difficult to find and is often a major expense, especially at peak times of the year – July and August, Easter and Christmas. Such is the popularity of Amsterdam as a short-break destination that you'd be well advised to make an advance reservation at any time of the year. In spite of this, most hotels only charge the full quoted rates at the very busiest times, which means that you'll often pay less than the peak-season prices for double rooms quoted in this book; it's certainly always worth asking if there is any discount available, especially on week nights when a lot of hotels routinely charge less anyway.

The Old Centre

BELLEVUE > Martelaarsgracht 10 ⊕ 020/707 4500, Ⓦ www .bellevuehotel.nl. MAP PP.34–35, POCKET MAP C10. All the rooms here are newly renovated in a modern style and the location couldn't be more convenient, two minutes from Centraal Station. Prices do not include breakfast. **€225**

GRAND HOTEL KRASNAPOLSKY > Dam 9 ⊕ 020/554 9111, Ⓦ www .nh-hotels.com. MAP PP.34–35, POCKET MAP B12. Located in a huge and striking mid-nineteenth-century building, this four-star hotel occupies virtually an entire side of Dam Square. Its rooms are nicely done, if unspectacular. Bargains are sometimes available. Breakfast not included. **€200**

HOTEL DES ARTS > Rokin 154–156 ⊕ 020/620 1558, Ⓦ www.hoteldesarts .nl. MAP PP.34–35, POCKET MAP B14. In a great location up near Muntplein, and very friendly. The more expensive rooms at the front are the ones to ask for in this moderately priced option. **€168**

HOTEL DE L'EUROPE > Nieuwe Doelenstraat 2–8 ⊕ 020/531 1777, Ⓦ www.leurope.nl. MAP PP.34–35, POCKET MAP B14. One of the city's top hotels, and retaining a wonderful fin-de-siècle charm, with large, well-furnished rooms, an attractive riverside terrace and a great central location. A canal view will cost you another €50 or so, but this is about as luxurious as the city gets. Breakfast not included. **€400**

LE COIN > Nieuwe Doelenstraat 5 ⊕ 020/524 6800, Ⓦ www.lecoin.nl. MAP PP.34–35, POCKET MAP B14. In a good location opposite the swanky *Hotel de l'Europe*, but a quarter of the price. All rooms have kitchenettes and are kitted out in contemporary fashion. **€139**

MISC > Kloveniersburgwal 20 ⊕ 020/330 6241, Ⓦ www.hotelmisc .com. MAP PP.34–35, POCKET MAP C12. Excellent, very friendly budget hotel on the edge of the Red Light District, with six good-sized rooms each with a different theme. Breakfast included. **€145**

NES > Kloveniersburgwal 137–139 ⊕ 020/624 4773, Ⓦ www.hotelnes. nl. MAP PP.34–35, POCKET MAP C14. Pleasant and quiet hotel with helpful staff, and well positioned away from noise but close to shops and nightlife. It's also recently been given a bit of a facelift so rooms and public areas are much more consistent than before. **€150**

Prices and tax

The least expensive hotels charge around €100 for a double room, a little less if you share a bathroom, but don't expect too much in the way of creature comforts at these sort of prices – you only really hit any sort of comfort zone at about €120-plus. Breakfast – bread, jam, eggs, ham and cheese – is often included in the price at the budget and moderately priced hotels, as is tax (five percent), but as ever the more expensive hotels slap both on top of quoted prices. One other thing to bear in mind: some of the cheaper hotels request full payment in advance or on arrival.

NH CITY CENTRE > Spuistraat 288 ☎ 020/420 4545, ⓦ www.nh-hotels .com. MAP PP.34–35, POCKET MAP A13. A chain hotel, but an appealing one, in a sympathetically renovated 1920s Art Deco former textile factory, and well situated for the cafés and bars of the Spui and around. Rooms vary in size, some have canal views, and all boast extremely comfy beds and good showers. Breakfast included. **€150**

RHO > Nes 5 ☎ 020/620 7371, ⓦ www .rhohotel.com. MAP PP.34–35, POCKET MAP B12. Built as a theatre in 1908, the lovely high-ceilinged, fin-de-siècle lobby gives a slightly misleading impression: the rooms are on the small side and have been unimaginatively modernized. Still, it's pleasant enough, and in a good central location just off Dam Square. Breakfast included. Daily bike rental available. **€115**

SINT NICOLAAS > Spuistraat 1a ☎ 020/626 1384, ⓦ www .hotelnicolaas.nl. MAP PP.34–35, POCKET MAP B11. Quirkier than many of the other budget hotels in the area, the St Nicolaas's cosy downstairs bar-reception gives way to around thirty rooms, all with baths. Conveniently located too, just five minutes' walk from Centraal Station. **€135**

VICTORIA > Damrak 1–5 ☎ 020/623 4255, ⓦ www.parkplaza.com. MAP PP.34–35, POCKET MAP C11. This tall, elegant building opposite Centraal Station has been one of the city's best hotels for years, although its decor is beginning to look fusty compared to the crop of sleek options that has arrived in recent years. Still, its location couldn't be more convenient, and there are often bargains

to be had in its well-kitted-out rooms; amenities include a fitness centre and pool. Breakfast not included. **€200**

VIJAYA > Oudezijds Voorburgwal 44 ☎ 020/626 9406, ⓦ www.hotelvijaya .com. MAP PP.34–35, POCKET MAP C11. Right in the heart of the Red Light District, next door but one to the Amstelkring (see p.40), this is a warren of rooms spread over a couple of old canal houses. It's rather threadbare but has a friendly charm that's only enhanced by the Indian restaurant downstairs. No lift. Ten minutes' walk from Centraal Station. **€95**

WINSTON > Warmoesstraat 129 ☎ 020/623 1380, ⓦ www.winston .nl. MAP PP.34–35, POCKET MAP C12. Part of the St Christopher's Inns chain, this self-consciously young and cool hotel has funky rooms individually decorated with crazy art, and a busy ground-floor bar that has regular live music. It's a formula that works a treat; the *Winston* is popular and often full – though this is probably also due to its low prices which include breakfast. Dorm beds available too, from around €30 a head during high season. Lift and full disabled access. Ten minutes' walk from Centraal Station. **€100**

Grachtengordel

AMBASSADE > Herengracht 341 ☎ 020/555 0222, ⓦ www .ambassade-hotel.nl. MAP PP.54–55, POCKET MAP A13. Elegant canalside hotel made up of ten seventeenth-century houses with smartly furnished lounges, a well-stocked library and comfortable en-suite rooms. Free 24hr internet access. Breakfast is an extra €16, but well worth it. **€195**

Booking hotels

You can obviously book direct online or by phone, or you can compare prices and availability through the usual accommodation booking engines; one specific to Amsterdam is that of the Amsterdam Tourism Board – Ⓦ www .amsterdamtourist.nl. Once you've arrived, the city's tourist offices (see p.135) will make on-the-spot hotel reservations on your behalf for a small fee, but during peak periods and weekends they get extremely busy with long and time-consuming queues. The good news is that the city's compactness means that you'll almost inevitably end up somewhere central.

AMSTERDAM AMERICAN > Leidsekade 97 Ⓣ 020/556 3000, Ⓦ www.amsterdamamerican.com. MAP PP.54–55, POCKET MAP B6. Landmark Art Deco hotel just off Leidseplein that dates from 1902, though the bedrooms themselves are mostly kitted out in standard modern style. Large, double-glazed doubles; breakfast not included. **€140**

BACKSTAGE HOTEL > Leidsegracht 114 Ⓣ 020624 4044, Ⓦ www .backstagehotel.nl. MAP PP.54–55, POCKET MAP B5. This hotel is aimed at musicians playing at the nearby *Melkweg* and *Paradiso*, and furnishings like theatre mirrors, spotlights and flight cases in the 22 rooms are designed to make them feel at home. Everyone can enjoy the free internet, 24hr bar and pool table. **€130**

CHIC & BASIC > Herengracht 13 Ⓣ 020/522 2345, Ⓦ www.chicandbasic .com. MAP PP.54–55, POCKET MAP B10. Dutch branch of this spunky Spanish concept, with 26 basic but cool rooms, some overlooking the canal. The changeable lighting allows you to adjust the colour of your room according to your mood – a cheapo gimmick, but an effective one. Breakfast not included. **€125**

CLEMENS > Raadhuisstraat 39 Ⓣ 020/624 6089, Ⓦ www .clemenshotel.nl. MAP PP.54–55, POCKET MAP C3. Well-run budget hotel in a good location close to the Anne Frank Huis, and one of the better options along this busy main road. Breakfast is extra. All rooms offer free internet, and you can rent laptops for just a few euros. Doubles with shower are more expensive. **€60**

DIKKER & THIJS FENICE > Prinsengracht 444 Ⓣ 020/620 1212, Ⓦ www.dtfh.nl. MAP PP.54–55, POCKET MAP C5. Small and stylish hotel not far from Leidseplein. Rooms vary in decor but all include a minibar, telephone and TV. Those on the top floor have good views of the city. Includes breakfast. **€125**

DYLAN > Keizersgracht 384 Ⓣ 020/530 2010, Ⓦ www .dylanamsterdam.com. MAP PP.54–55, POCKET MAP C4. This stylish hotel is housed in a seventeenth-century building that centres on a beautiful courtyard and terrace. Its 41 sumptuous rooms range in style from opulent reds or greens to minimal white decor, and have flat-screen TVs and stereos. The restaurant combines French and African cuisine and the bar is open to non-guests. Luxury suites overlooking the Keizersgracht canal will set you back €1500. Breakfast is €24 extra. **€420**

ESTHEREA > Singel 303–309 Ⓣ 020/624 5146, Ⓦ www.estherea .nl. MAP PP.54–55, POCKET MAP A13. Comfortable four-star converted from a couple of sympathetically modernized canal houses. There's no hankering after minimalism here, with thick, plush carpets and beds that you literally sink into. Excludes breakfast. **€260**

HEGRA > Herengracht 269 Ⓣ 020/623 7877, Ⓦ www.hotelhegra.nl. MAP PP.54–55, POCKET MAP A13. This family-run hotel has a welcoming atmosphere and is pretty good value considering the location, on a handsome stretch of canal near the Spui. Rooms are small but comfortable, whether en suite or with shared facilities. Breakfast included. €95

'T HOTEL > Leliegracht 18 ☎ 020/422 2741, ⓦ www.amsterdamby.com /thotel. MAP PP.54–55, POCKET MAP A11. Appealing hotel located in an old high-gabled house along a quiet stretch of canal. The eight spacious rooms are decorated in bright, modern style with large beds and either bath or shower. No groups. Minimum three-night stay at the weekend; includes breakfast. €125

HOTEL 717 > Prinsengracht 717 ☎ 020/427 0717, ⓦ www.717hotel.nl. MAP PP.54–55, POCKET MAP C5. Very exclusive canal house hotel with just eight suites, all individually designed. Great, large spaces, beautifully conceived, and perhaps the most luxurious small hotel in the city. €400

DE LEYDSCHE HOF > Leidsegracht 14 ☎ 020/638 2327, ⓦ www.freewebs .com/leydschehof. MAP PP.54–55, POCKET MAP C5. Just seven rooms in this handsome canal house in a great location on the Leidsegracht between Herengracht and Keizersgracht. Simple but comfy, and very welcoming. €120

MARCEL'S CREATIVE EXCHANGE > Leidsestraat 87 ☎ 020/622 9834, ⓦ www.marcelamsterdam.com. MAP PP.54–55, POCKET MAP C5. Popular B&B run by an English-speaking graphic designer and artist who attracts like-minded people to this stylishly restored house with four en-suite doubles available for two, three or four people sharing. Decor is chic and comfortable. Relaxing and peaceful amid the buzz of the city. You'll need to book well in advance in high season. Breakfast isn't included, but there are tea- and coffee-making facilities. €120

OP DE GRACHT > Prinsengracht 826 ☎ 020/626 1937, ⓦ www.opdegracht .nl. MAP PP.54–55, POCKET MAP E6. This B&B, run by the very pleasant Jolanda Schipper, is in a good-looking old house on one of the main canals. The two rooms are tastefully decorated, both with en-suite bathrooms. Minimum stay two nights. €90

PRINSENHOF > Prinsengracht 810 ☎ 020/623 1772, ⓦ www .hotelprinsenhof.com. MAP PP.54–55, POCKET MAP E6. Tastefully decorated, this is one of the city's top budget options. Booking essential. Tram #4 from Centraal Station to Prinsengracht. Cheaper rooms without shower. €85

REMBRANDT SQUARE HOTEL > Rembrandtplein 24 ☎ 020/620 0652, ⓦ www.rembrandtsquarehotel.com. Cheerful one-star hotel with an urban feel, located just off the busy Rembrandtplein. Rooms are all well equipped and tastefully decorated in various colourful shades. Tram #4 or #9 to Rembrandtplein. €70

SEVEN BRIDGES > Reguliersgracht 31 ☎ 020/623 1329, ⓦ www .sevenbridgeshotel.nl. MAP PP.54–55, POCKET MAP E5. Very charming place – and excellent value for money. It takes its name from its canalside location, which affords a view of seven dinky little bridges. Beautifully decorated in an antique style, its spotless rooms are regularly revamped. Small and popular, so reservations are pretty much essential. Breakfast is included in the price and served in your room. Trams #16, #24 or #25 from Centraal Station to Keizersgracht. €110

THE TIMES HOTEL > Herengracht 135 ☎ 020/330 6030, ⓦ www .thetimeshotel.nl. MAP PP.54–55, POCKET MAP A11. Colourful designer hotel with a wink to the old Dutch masters – it's decked out with reproductions of paintings by Rembrandt, Vermeer et al. in every room. Good location, and free wi-fi. Excludes breakfast. €159

TOREN > Keizersgracht 164 ☎ 020/622 6033, ⓦ www.hoteltoren .nl. MAP PP.54–55, POCKET MAP C3. Retro-chic boutique hotel, converted from two elegant canal houses. All rooms have been renovated, some have large jacuzzis and there's also an annexe. There's a breakfast room downstairs and they offer an adapted menu from nearby *Christophe* restaurant if you want to eat in the evening. €200

WIECHMANN > Prinsengracht 328–332 ☎020/626 3321, ⓦwww.hotelwiechmann.nl. MAP PP.54–55, POCKET MAP C4. Family-run for over fifty years, this hotel occupies an attractively restored canal house close to the Anne Frank Huis, with dark wooden beams and restrained style throughout. Large, bright rooms are in perfect condition with TV and shower. **€140**

The Jordaan and the Western docklands

ACACIA > Lindengracht 251 ☎020/622 1460, ⓦwww.hotelacacia.nl. MAP P.73, POCKET MAP B2. Small hotel situated in the heart of the Jordaan, right on a corner, so some of the rooms have wide views of the canal and its adjoining streets. Rooms, which sleep two to four people, are rather nondescript with small beds and a shower room. There are also self-catering studios (€90). Includes breakfast. **€80**

VAN ONNA > Bloemgracht 102 ☎020/626 5801, ⓦwww.otelvanonna.nl. MAP P.73, POCKET MAP B3. A quiet, well-maintained place on a tranquil canal. The building dates back over three hundred years and still retains some of its original fixtures, though the rooms themselves are rather modest, with basic furniture and blankets on beds. Simple setup – no TV, no smoking and cash payment only. Booking advised. Includes breakfast. **€90**

The Old Jewish Quarter and the Eastern docklands

ADOLESCE > Nieuwe Keizersgracht 26 ☎020/626 3959, ⓦwww.adolesce.nl. MAP PP.82–83, POCKET MAP F5. Popular and welcoming no-frills hotel in an old canal house not far from Waterlooplein. There are ten neat and trim modern rooms and a large dining room. No breakfast. Triples are also available. **€95**

LLOYD HOTEL > Oostelijke Handelskade 34 ☎020/561 3636, ⓦwww.lloydhotel.com. MAP PP.82–83, POCKET MAP H3. Situated in the up-and-coming Oosterdok district, this ex-prison and migrant workers' hostel has been renovated to become Amsterdam's coolest hotel. Rather pretentiously subtitled a "cultural embassy", it has an arts centre too, with regular exhibitions, readings and performances, an art library, and a nice, bustling feel that revolves around its airy central restaurant and lobby area on the ground floor. Uniquely it serves all kinds of travellers, with rooms ranging from one-star affairs to five-star offerings. Some rooms are great, others not so – don't be afraid to ask to change. The location is better than you might think – just five minutes' by tram #26 from Centraal Station but at these prices you still might prefer to be in the centre. One-star **€100**, five-star, **€320**

The Museum Quarter and the Vondelpark

ACRO > Jan Luykenstraat 44 ☎020/662 5538, ⓦwww.acro-hotel.nl. MAP P.96, POCKET MAP B6. This hotel has small and functional rooms, but the friendly welcome and nice bar on the ground floor mean that it gets booked up a long way in advance. Wi-fi and bicycle rent available. Breakfast included. **€100**

BILDERBERG HOTEL JAN LUYKEN > Jan Luykenstraat 58 ☎020/573 0730, ⓦwww.janluyken.nl. MAP P.96, POCKET MAP B6. Good-sized, nicely refurbished rooms mark out this decent stab at a mini four-star, full-service hotel. There's wi-fi in rooms, 24hr room service and a nice lounge and bar too. **€130**

COLLEGE > Roelof Hartstraat 1 ☎020/571 1511, ⓦwww.collegehotelamsterdam.com. MAP P.96, POCKET MAP C8. Converted from an old schoolhouse, the *College* is one of the most elegant and original additions to Amsterdam's hotel scene. Original because it's largely run by students from the city's catering school; elegant because of the sheer class of the refurbishment. €200

FILOSOOF > Anna van den Vondelstraat 6 ☎020/683 3013, ⓦwww.sandton.eu/nl/amsterdaml. MAP P.96, POCKET MAP A6. A lovely small hotel, with each room decorated according to a different philosophical theme. It's all beautifully kept, nothing is too much trouble, and the garden outside is a rare Amsterdam treat. A bit of the way but handy for the Vondelpark. Breakfast included. €160

OWL HOTEL > Roemer Visscherstraat 1 ☎020/618 9484, ⓦwww.owl-hotel.nl. MAP P.96, POCKET MAP B6. The reasonably priced doubles are relatively blandly furnished, but its location is nice and quiet, with a downstairs lounge opening onto a lovely garden, and – run by the same family for nearly forty years – the staff are a welcoming bunch. €130

PIET HEIN > Vossiusstraat 53 ☎020/662 7205, ⓦwww.hotelpiethein.nl. MAP P.96, POCKET MAP B6. Five minutes' walk from Leidseplein, this sleek three-star has large rooms with views over the entrance to the Vondelpark and slightly more expensive rooms in the modern annexe overlooking its peaceful back garden. There's also a comfy bar that's open till 1am. Lift access. €135

ROEMER > Roemer Visscherstraat 10 ☎020/515 0455, ⓦwww.hotelroemer.nl. MAP P.96, POCKET MAP B6. Sister hotel of the excellent *Vondel* and just as slick and stylish, this boutique hotel has a very pleasant garden out the back. Decor is funky and fun, with colourful paintings on the walls, sleek bathrooms and comfortable beds. €200

TORO > Koningslaan 64 ☎020/673 7223, ⓦwww.hoteltoro.nl. MAP P.96, POCKET MAP A7. In a grand old villa overlooking the Vondelpark's westerly reaches, this hotel is like a small country house, with a comfy downstairs sitting room and attractive rooms, some of which overlook the park. A nice choice if you don't mind being slightly out of the action. €150

VONDEL > Vondelstraat 18–30 ☎020/616 4075, ⓦwww.hotelvondel.com. MAP P.96, POCKET MAP B6. Part of a small chain of design-conscious boutique hotels that is beginning to dominate this part of the city, this place is as cool as its cousins, with has black paint and light natural wood characterizing the lovely rooms, which have flatscreen TVs. There's a pleasant bar and breakfast room and modern art decorates the walls of the common areas. Doubles vary in size. €160

The Outer Districts

HOTEL ARENA > 's-Gravesandestraat 51 ☎020/850 2400, ⓦwww.hotelarena.nl. MAP PP.82–83, POCKET MAP H6. A little way east of the centre, in a renovated old convent on the edge of the Oosterpark, this place has been thoroughly revamped, transforming a popular hostel into a hip three-star hotel complete with split-level rooms and minimalist decor. Despite the odd pretentious flourish, it manages to retain a relaxed vibe attracting both businesspeople and travellers alike. Lively bar, intimate restaurant, and late-night club (Fri & Sat) located within the former chapel. €110

HOTEL OKURA > Ferdinand Bolstraat 333 ☎020/678 7111, ⓦwww.okura.nl. MAP PP.104–105, POCKET MAP D9. Don't be fooled by the concrete, purpose-built facade: this deluxe five-star hotel comes equipped with all the luxuries you would expect, such as a health club and sauna, and even a shopping arcade with a Japanese food store. Rooms have huge marble bathrooms, and, in the suites, mood lighting and control units for the curtains. Two of its four restaurants (see p.110) have Michelin stars. If you're feeling flush you could book "The Suite", set over two floors with a suspended glass staircase, private butler and cinema; a night here will set you back €10,000. €315

VAN OSTADE > Van Ostadestraat 123
☎020/679 3452, Ⓦwww.bicyclehotel.com.
MAP PP.104–105, POCKET MAP D8.
Friendly place down a quiet residential
street, not far from Albert Cuyp market
in De Pijp. It bills itself as the "bicycle
hotel", renting bikes for €7.50 per
day and giving advice on routes and
suchlike. Garage parking for two cars
(€20), though you'll need to book in
advance. Basic but clean two-, three-
and four-bed rooms come with shared
facilities, and rates include breakfast.
Tram #25 from Centraal Station to 1e
van de Helststraat. **€75**

XAVIERA HOLLANDER B&B >
Stadionweg 7 ☎020/673 3934. Ⓦwww
.xavierhollander.com MAP P.96, POCKET
MAP B9. A bit out of the way in the
chi-chi New South, but this B&B, run
by ex-prostitute Xaviera Hollander, is
a real Amsterdam experience, with a
couple of kitschy rooms kitted out with
semi-clad photos of the owner and lots of
well-thumbed sex manuals. Both rooms
have shared facilities, but it's still very
comfortable and welcoming. **€110**

Hostels

The least expensive central option is to take a dormitory bed
in a hostel – and there are plenty to choose from: Hostelling
International places, unofficial private hostels, even Christian
hostels. Most hostels will either provide (relatively) clean
bed linen or charge a few euros for it, though frankly your
own sleeping bag might be a better option. Many hostels also
lock guests out for a short period each day to clean the place,
and some set a nightly curfew, though these are usually late
enough not to cause too much of a problem. Note that many
hostels don't accept reservations from June to August.

The Old Centre

BOB'S YOUTH HOSTEL > Nieuwezijds
Voorburgwal 92 ☎ 020/623 0063,
Ⓦ www.bobshostel.nl. MAP PP.34–35,
POCKET MAP D3. An old favourite with
backpackers, *Bob's* is a lively place with
small, basic dorm beds for around €20
per person, including breakfast in the
coffeeshop on the ground floor. They also
let four apartments (€70 for two people,
€80 for three). Just 10 minutes' walk
from Amsterdam Centraal Station.

BULLDOG LOW-BUDGET HOTEL >
Oudezijds Voorburgwal 220 ☎020/620
3822, Ⓦwww.bulldoghotel.com. MAP
PP.34–35, POCKET MAP E3. Part of the
Bulldog coffeeshop chain, with a bar

and DVD lounge downstairs complete
with leather couches and soft lighting.
Dorm beds with TV and shower start
at €27, including breakfast, and there
are also double bunks available and
rooms for €90, as well as fully equipped
apartments from €130 – all with
bathrooms and TVs. Trams #4, #9, #16
or #24 from Centraal Station to Dam
Square, then a 3min walk.

FLYING PIG DOWNTOWN Nieuwendijk
100 > ☎ 020/420 6822, Ⓦwww
.flyingpig.nl. MAP PP.34–35, POCKET
MAP C11. Clean, large and well run by
ex-travellers familiar with the needs of
backpackers. Free use of kitchen facilities,
no curfew, there's a late-night coffeeshop
next door and the hostel bar is open all

night. Justifiably popular, and a very good deal, with mixed dorm beds from just €20 depending on the size of the dorm. Just a 5min walk from Centraal Station.

STAY OKAY > Stadsdoelen Kloveniersburgwal 97 ☏ 020/624 6832, Ⓦ www.stayokay.com/stadsdoelen. MAP PP.34–35, POCKET MAP C13. The closest to Centraal Station of the two official hostels, with clean, semi-private dorms at €20 for members, who get priority in high season; non-members pay €23.50. Price includes linen, breakfast and locker, plus use of communal kitchen. The bar overlooks the canal and serves good-value if basic food, and there's a 2am curfew (though the door opens for three 15min intervals between 2am and 7am). Metro Nieuwmarkt, or trams #4, #9, #16, #24 or #25 from Centraal Station to Muntplein. See also the city's other HI hostel, the *Stay Okay Vondelpark* (see below), which has a greater choice of rooms.

Grachtengordel

HANS BRINKER > Kerkstraat 136 ☏ 020/622 0687, Ⓦ www.hans-brinker .com. MAP PP.54–55, POCKET MAP C5. Well-established and raucously popular Amsterdam hostel, with around 600 beds. Dorms are basic and clean and beds go for €25 and upwards, and en-suite singles, doubles and triples are also available for €40 a head. The facilities are good: free internet after 10pm, disco every night, and it's near to the buzz of Leidseplein too. A hostel to head for if you're out for a good time (and not too bothered about getting a solid night's sleep). Walk-in policy only. Trams #1, #2 or #5 from Centraal Station to Prinsengracht.

INTERNATIONAL BUDGET HOTEL > Leidsegracht 76 ☏ 020/624 2784, Ⓦ www.internationalbudgethostel .com. MAP PP.54–55, POCKET MAP B5. An excellent budget option on a peaceful little canal in the heart of the city. Small, simple rooms sleeping up to four with shared facilities cost around €25–30 a head during summer and twin rooms

Our picks

BUDGET *Seven Bridges* > p.123
CENTRAL *Estherea* > p.122
BOUTIQUE *Vondel* > p.125
ROMANCE *Toren* > p.123
CELEBS *Dylan* > p.122
LUXURY *717* > p.123
GRUNGY *Winston* > p.121

€130–160. Young, friendly staff. Trams #1, #2 or #5 to Prinsengracht.

The Museum Quarter and the Vondelpark

FLYING PIG UPTOWN > Vossiusstraat 46 ☏ 020/400 4187, Ⓦ www.flyingpig .nl. MAP P.96, POCKET MAP B6. The better of the two *Flying Pig* hostels (see opposite), facing the Vondelpark and close to the city's most important museums. Immaculate and well maintained by a staff of travellers, who understand their backpacking guests. Free use of kitchen facilities, no curfew and good tourist information. Fourteen-bed dorms start at €14.90 per person and there are a few two-person queensize bunks, as well as double rooms(€31.90). Great value. Trams #1, #2 or #5 from Centraal Station to Leidseplein, then walk.

STAY OKAY VONDELPARK > Zandpad 5 ☏ 020/589 8996, Ⓦ www .stayokay.com/vondelpark. MAP P.96, POCKET MAP B6. The better of the city's two HI hostels, with a bar, restaurant, TV lounge, internet access and bike shed, plus various discount facilities for tours and museums. Rates start at €20 per person in a shared dorm, including use of all facilities, shower, sheets and breakfast, but there are private rooms too (€95). Secure lockers and no curfew. To be sure of a place in high season you'll need to book at least two months ahead. Trams #1, #2 or #5 from Centraal Station to Leidseplein, then walk.

ESSENTIALS

Arrival

Arriving in Amsterdam by train and plane could hardly be easier. Amsterdam's international **airport** is a quick and convenient train ride away from the city's **international train station**, which is itself just a ten-minute metro ride from the terminus for long-distance and international buses.

By air

Amsterdam's international airport, **Schiphol** (☎ 0900/0141, ⓦ www .schiphol.nl), is located about 15km southwest of the city centre. Trains run from there to Amsterdam Centraal Station every ten minutes during the day, every hour at night (midnight–6am); the journey takes 15–20 minutes and costs €3.80 each. Taxi fares from Schiphol to most parts of the city centre are €40–45. The Connexxion bus service (☎ 038/339 4741, ⓦ www .schipholhotelshuttle.nl) departs from the designated bus stop outside the Arrivals Hall every half an hour (on the half-hour) from 6am to 9pm at a cost of €13.50 one-way, €22 return. The route varies with the needs of the passengers it picks up at the airport, but buses take about thirty minutes to get from the airport to the city centre. Tickets are available from the Connexxion desk in the Arrivals Hall.

By train

Amsterdam's **Centraal Station** (CS) has regular connections with key cities in Germany, Belgium and France, as well as all the larger towns and cities of the Netherlands. Amsterdam also has several suburban train stations, but these are principally for commuters. For all rail enquiries contact **NS** (Netherlands Railways; international enquiries ☎ 0900/9296;

domestic enquiries ☎ 0900/9292; ⓦ www.ns.nl or ⓦ www.9292ov.nl).

By bus

Eurolines (☎ 020/560 8788, ⓦ www .eurolines.nl) long-distance, international buses arrive at Amstel Station, about 3.5km to the southeast of Centraal Station. The metro journey to Centraal Station takes about ten minutes.

City transport

Almost all of Amsterdam's leading attractions are within easy walking distance of each other. The city has a first-rate public transport system, run by the **GVB**. Centraal Station is the hub of the system, with trams and buses departing from outside on Stationsplein, which is also the location of a metro station and a GVB public transport information office. There's a taxi rank on Stationsplein too.

Tickets

The **OV-Chipkaart** (ⓦ www .ov-chipkaart.nl) is an electronic payment card which covers the cost of travelling on all of the GVB transport system. There are two main sorts of card – rechargeable plastic cards and disposable paper cards set to a pre-determined value and length of time. They are sold at the tourist office and on the city's trams and at the metro. You must scan the card when you get on and off the bus, tram, ferry or metro. The cheapest card, a one-hour paper card, costs €2.60. A disposable *dagkaart* (day ticket), for unlimited travel, costs €7 for 24 hours, €11.50 for 48 hours and €15.50 for 72 hours. Note that the GVB tries hard to keep fare-dodging to a minimum, and wherever you're travelling and at whatever time of day, there's a chance you'll have your ticket checked. If you are caught without a valid ticket, you risk an on-the-spot fine of €35.

Trams, metro and buses

Trams crisscross the city: two of the most useful are #2 and #5, which link Centraal Station with Leidsestraat and the Rijksmuseum every ten minutes or so during the day. **Buses** are mainly useful for going to the outskirts, and the same applies to the **metro**, which has just two city centre stations, Nieuwmarkt and Waterlooplein. Trams, buses and the metro operate daily between 6am and midnight, supplemented by a limited number of nightbuses (*nachtbussen*). All tram and bus stops display a detailed map of the network. For further details on all services, head for the main GVB information office (Mon–Fri 7am–9pm, Sat & Sun 10am–6pm; ☎ 0900/8011, ⊛ www .gvb.nl) on Stationsplein. Its free, English-language *Tourist Guide to Public Transport* is very helpful, and it provides free transport maps too.

The Canal Bus

One good way to get around Amsterdam's waterways is to take the **Canal Bus** (☎ 020/623 9886, ⊛ www.canal.nl). This operates on three circular routes, coloured green, red and blue, which meet at various places: at the jetty opposite Centraal Station beside Prins Hendrikkade; on the Singelgracht (opposite the Rijksmuseum), near the Leidseplein; and by the Stadhuis on Waterlooplein. There are fourteen stops in all and together they give easy access to all the major sights. Boats leave from opposite Centraal Station every half an hour or so during low season between 10am and 5.30pm (longer in high

season), and a 24hr ticket for all three routes, allowing you to hop on and off as many times as you like, costs €22 per adult, €11 for children (4–11 years old). The ticket also entitles the bearer to minor discounts at several museums. Two-day passes cost €33.

Hop On Hop Off

A similar boat service, the **Hop On Hop Off** (☎ 020/530 5412, ⊛ www.lovers.nl), has two routes, with either seven stops or nine stops located located at or near many of the city's major attractions. It departs from opposite Centraal Station (10 daily between 10am–5pm, every 30min on Sat) and a hop-on-hop-off day ticket costs €18.50, children €10 (4–12 years old).

Boat tours

There are several **boat tour** operators and they occupy the prime pitches – the jetties near Centraal Station on Stationsplein, beside the Damrak and on Prins Hendrikkade. **Prices** are fairly uniform with a one-hour tour costing around €11 per adult, €6 per child (4–12 years old), and around €25 (€15) for a two-hour cruise at night. The big companies also offer more **specialized boat trips** – dinner cruises from around €55, literary cruises, and most notably the weekly Historical Cruise run by Lovers (☎ 020/530 5412, ⊛ www.lovers.nl; €17–30). All these cruises are popular and long queues are common in the summer. One way of avoiding much of the crush is to walk down the Damrak from Centraal Station to the jetty at the near end of the Rokin, where the first-rate Reederij P. Kooij (who also have a jetty beside Centraal Station) offers all the basic cruises at competitive prices.

Canal Bikes

You can rent **Canal Bikes** (☎ 020/626 5574, ⊛ www.canal.nl) – four-seater

Tour operators

Mee in Mokum Keizersgracht 346 ☎ 020/625 1390, ⌨ meeinmokum.nl Guided walking tours of the old centre and the Jordaan by long-time – and often older – Amsterdam residents. Tours run four or five times weekly; €5 per person. Advance reservations required.

Reederij P. Kooij on the Rokin, beside the Queen Wilhelmina statue ☎ 020/623 3810, ⌨ www.rederijkooij.nl. Provides a range of cruises by day and by night, at prices that are often cheaper than the rest. Also has a (more crowded) jetty opposite Centraal Station on Stationsplein.

Yellow Bike Tours Nieuwezijds Kolk 29, off Nieuwezijds Voorburgwal ☎ 020/620 6940, ⌨ www.yellowbike.nl. Three-hour guided cycling tours around the city (2 daily) that cost €21.50 per person, including the bike. Advance reservations required.

pedaloes – at four central locations: on the Singelgracht opposite the Rijks-museum; the Prinsengracht outside the Anne Frankhuis; on Keizersgracht at Leidsestraat; and behind Leidseplein. Rental prices per person per hour are €7 (3–4 people) or €8 (1–2 people), plus a refundable deposit of €50. They can be picked up at one location and left at any of the others; opening times are April to October daily 10am to 6pm, until 9.30pm in July and August.

Bicycles

The city has an excellent network of designated bicycle lanes (*fietspaden*). The needs of the cyclist often take precedence over those of the motorist and by law, if there's a collision, it's always the driver's fault.

Bike rental is straightforward. There are lots of **rental compa-nies** (*fietsenverhuur*) but MacBike (daily 9am–5.45pm; ☎ 020/624 8391, ⌨ www.macbike.nl) is perhaps the most convenient, with three rental outlets in central Amsterdam: one at the east end of Centraal Station,

a second beside Waterlooplein at Mr Visserplein 2, and a third near Leidseplein at Weteringschans 2. They charge €7 for three hours, €9.50 per day, €19 for three days and €30.80 for a week for a standard bicycle; 21-speed cycles cost about half as much again. All companies ask for some type of security, usually in the form of a cash deposit (some will take credit card imprints) and/or passport.

Taxis

The centre of Amsterdam is geared up for trams and bicycles rather than cars, so **taxis** are not as much use as they are in many other cities. They are, however, plentiful: taxi ranks are all over the city centre and they can also be hailed on the street. **Fares** are metered and reasonably high, but distances are small: the trip from Centraal Station to the Leidseplein, for example, will cost around €12, €2 more to Museumplein – and about fifteen percent more late at night.

Directory A–Z

Addresses

Addresses are written as, for example, "Kerkstr.79 II", which means the second-floor apartment at Kerstraat 79. The ground floor is indicated by *hs* (huis, house) after the number; the basement is *sous* (souterrain). In some cases 1e, 2e, 3e and even occasionally 4e are placed in front; these are abbreviations for *Eersete* (first), *Tweede* (second), *Derde* (third) and *Vierde* (fourth). Many side streets take the name of the street they run off, with the addition of the word *dwars*, meaning "'crossing"' – for instance, Palmdwarsstraat is a side street off Palmstraat. The main Grachtengordel canals begin their numbering at Brouwersgracht and increase as they progress anticlockwise. T/O (tegenover or "opposite") in an address shows that the address is a boat.

Cinema

Most of Amsterdam's commercial **cinemas** are multiplexes showing general releases, but there's also a scattering of film houses showing revival and art films and occasional retrospectives. The **Kriterion** at Roeterstraat 170 (☎ 020/623 1708, ⓦ www.kriterion.nl) is a stylish cinema close to Weesperplein metro that shows arthouse and quality commercial films, while the beautiful Art Deco cinema **The Movies**, at Haarlemmerdijk 161 (☎ 020/63806016, ⓦ www.themovies .nl), shows independent films.

Drugs

All **soft drugs** – as well as hard – are technically illegal, but possession and consumption have been partly decriminalized. Under no circumstances should you take cannabis out of the country. **"Space cakes"** (cakes baked with hashish and sold by the slice), although widely available, count as hard drugs and are illegal.

Electricity

The Dutch electricity supply runs at 220V AC.British equipment needs only a plug adaptor; American apparatus requires a transformer and an adaptor.

Embassies and consulates

Australia Carnegielaan 4, The Hague ☎ 070/310 8200; **Canada** Sophialaan 2514 JP The Hague ☎ 070/311 1600; **Ireland** Dr Kuijperstraat 9, 2514 BA The Hague ☎ 070/363 0993; **New Zealand** Eisenhowerlaan 77, 2517 KK The Hague ☎ 070/346 9324; **South Africa** Wassenaarseweg 40, 2596 CJ The Hague ☎ 070/392 4501; **UK** Lange Voorhout 10, 2514 ED The Hague ☎ 070/427 0427; **USA** Lange Voorhout 102, 2514 EJ The Hague ☎ 070/310 2209.

Gay and lesbian Amsterdam

Amsterdam is one of the top gay destinations in Europe: attitudes are tolerant, bars are excellent and plentiful, and support groups and facilities are unequalled. The age of consent is 16. For help and advice contact the Gay & Lesbian Switchboard ☎ 020/623 6565, ⓦ www .switchboard.nl (Mon–Fri noon–10pm, Sat & Sun 4–8pm). Consider timing your visit to coincide with Amsterdam Pride (ⓦ www.amsterdamgapride. nl) on the first weekend of August or Leather Pride (ⓦ www.leatherpride.nl) in late October and November.

Health

Your hotel or the VVV should be able to provide the address of an English-speaking doctor or dentist if you need one. Otherwise call the emergency number ☎ 112. **Minor ailments** can be remedied at a drugstore (drogist). These sell non-prescription drugs as well as toiletries, tampons, condoms and the like. A pharmacy or *apotheek* (usually open Mon–Fri 9.30am–6pm, but often closed Mon mornings) also handles prescriptions; centrally located pharmacies includes Dam Apotheek (Damstraat 2 ☎ 020/624 4331), Lairesse Apotheek (De Lairesseestraat 40 ☎ 020/662 1022) and Apotheek Koek, Schaeffer & Van Tijen (Vijzelgracht 19 ☎ 020/623 5949).

Internet

Most hotels provide internet access or wi-fi to guests either free, or at a minimal charge. A central internet café is *Internetcafe* at Martelaarsgracht 11 (daily 9am–1am, Fri & Sat until 3am; ☒ www.internetcafe.nl), just 200m from Centraal Station.

Left luggage

Centraal Station has coin-operated luggage lockers (daily 7am–11pm) and a staffed left-luggage office (daily 7am–11pm).

Lost property

For items lost on the trams, buses or metro, contact GVB Head Office, Prins Hendrikkade 108–114 (Mon–Fri 6.30am–11pm, Sat & Sun 8am–11pm; ☎ 0900/8011). For property lost on a train, go to the Gevonden Voorwerpen office at the nearest station; Amsterdam's is at Centraal Station, near the left-luggage lockers.

Mail

By 2012, all postal transactions will be carried out at the new TNT stores or places with the TNT logo. Stamps are sold at supermarkets, shops and hotels.

Emergency numbers

For the police, fire service and ambulance call ☎ 112.

Money

Debit cards are now the norm, and most shops and restaurants accept these and all major credit cards. You'll find ATMs throughout the city. Bureaux de change are also scattered around town – GWK has 24-hour branches at Centraal Station and Schiphol airport. The VVV tourist office also changes money. For **lost** and **stolen** credit cards and travellers' cheques the relevant numbers are: American Express ☎ 020/504 8666; Mastercard ☎ 0800 200 5821; Visa ☎ 0800 022 3110.

Opening hours

The Dutch weekend fades painlessly into the working week, with many smaller shops and businesses staying closed on Monday mornings til noon. Normal opening hours are, however, Monday to Friday 8.30am/9am to 5.30/6pm and Saturday 8.30/9am to 4/5pm. Many places also open late on Thursday or Friday evenings. Sunday opening is becoming increasingly common, especially within the city centre, where most shops are now open between noon and 5pm.

Most **restaurants** are open for dinner from about 6 or 7pm, and though many close as early as 9.30pm, a few stay open past 11pm. Bars, cafés and coffeeshops are either open all day from around 10am or don't open until about 5pm; all close at 1am during the week and 2am at weekends. Nightclubs generally open their doors from 11pm to 4am during the week, though a few open every night, and some stay open until 5am at the weekend. **Museums** are usually open from Monday to Friday from 10am to 5pm and from 11am to 5pm on weekends. Galleries tend to be open from Tuesday to Sunday from noon to 5pm.

Phones

The international phone code for the Netherlands is 31. Numbers prefixed ☎ 0800 are free; those prefixed ☎ 0900 are premium-rate – a (Dutch) message before you're connected tells you how much you will be paying for the call, and you can only call them from within the Netherlands. Phone booths are rapidly disappearing but there is a light scattering at major locations, like Centraal Station. **Phone cards** can be bought at outlets like tobacconists and VVV offices, and in several denominations, beginning at €5. The cheap-rate period for international calls is between 8pm and 8am during the week and all day at weekends. There is good coverage for **mobile phones/ cell phones** all over Amsterdam. Pre-paid SIM cards are available in telephone shops (on the Rokin and around Kalverstraat) and in some supermarkets. To speak to the operator (domestic and international), call ☎ 0800 0410; for directory enquiries, dial ☎ 0900 8008 (domestic), ☎ 0900 8418 (international). The Dutch phone directory is available (in Dutch) at ⓦ www.detelefoongids.nl.

Smoking

Smoking (tobacco) is banned in all public places as well as in all restaurants, cafés and bars and even coffeshops (see also p.000).

Time

The Netherlands is one hour behind UK time and 6 hours behind EST in the USA.

Tipping

You are expected to leave a tip if you have enjoyed good service – up to around ten percent of the bill should suffice in most restaurants, while hotel porters and taxi drivers may expect a euro or two on top of the fare.

Tourist information

There are two tourist offices – **VVVs** (pronounced "fay-fay-fay") – one on platform 2 at Centraal Station (daily 9am–7pm), and a second larger one across from the main station entrance on Stationsplein (Mon–Fri 9am–6pm, Sat & Sun 10am–6pm). The two offices share one website at ⓦ www.iamsterdam.com. They sell a range of maps and guide books as well as tickets and passes for public transport. They also take in-person bookings for canal cruises and other organized excursions, sell theatre and concert tickets, and operate an accommodation reservation service.

Tourist passes include the **Iamsterdam Card** (ⓦ iamsterdam.com) which provides free and unlimited use of the city's public transport network, a complimentary canal cruise and free admission to the bulk of the city's museums and attractions. It costs €38 for one day, €48 for two consecutive days and €58 for three consecutive days. It's not a bad deal, but you have to work fairly hard to make it worthwhile. It's available from any branch of the VVV.

An alternative if you're staying for more than a couple of days is the **Museumkaart** (ⓦ museumkart. nl), which gives free entry to almost every museum in the whole of the Netherlands for a year; it costs €35, or €17.50 for under-25s.

For information about what's on in the city, there's either the VVV or the **Amsterdam Uitburo**, the cultural office of the city council, housed in a corner of the Stadsschouwburg theatre on Leidseplein (Mon–Sat 10am–7.30pm, Sun noon–7.30pm; ☎ 020/795 9950). Listings magazines include the AUB's own monthly *Uitkrant*, which is comprehensive and free but in Dutch, or the VVV's *Day by Day in Amsterdam*.

Festivals and events

STILLE OMGANG (SILENT PROCESSION)

Sun closest to March 15 Ⓦ www .stille-omgang.nl.

Procession by local Catholics commemorating the Miracle of Amsterdam, starting and finishing at Spui.

KONINGINNEDAG (QUEEN'S DAY)

April 30

The highlight of the festival calendar: in celebration of Queen Beatrix's birthday, the entire city centre is given over to one massive party.

HERDENKINGSDAG (REMEMBRANCE DAY)/

May 4

Wreath-laying ceremony and two-minute silence at the National Monument in Dam Square, commemorating the Dutch dead of World War II.

BEVRIJDINGSDAG (LIBERATION DAY)

May 5

The country celebrates the 1945 liberation from Nazi occupation with bands, speeches and impromptu markets around the city.

Public holidays

January 1 New Year's Day
Good Friday (although shops open)
Easter Sunday
Easter Monday
April 30 Queen's Day
May 5 Liberation Day
Ascension Day
Whit Sunday and Monday
December 25 and 26 Christmas

HOLLAND FESTIVAL

Throughout June Ⓦ www.hollandfestival.nl.

The largest music, dance and drama event in the Netherlands, showcasing productions at venues around the city.

VONDELPARK OPEN AIR THEATRE

June–Aug Thurs–Sun only Ⓦ www .openluchttheater.nl.

Free theatre, dance and music performances throughout the summer, presenting anything from jazz and classical concerts through to stand-up comedy. The future existence of the theatre was uncertain at the time of writing, as its city government subsidy was under debate.

JULIDANS

First half of July Ⓦ www.julidans.nl.

Twelve- day festival dedicated to contemporary dance. It is held in numerous locations around the Leidseplein, with the Stadsschouwburg as its throbbing heart.

AMSTERDAM PRIDE

First or second weekend in Aug Ⓦ www .amsterdampride.nl.

The city's gay community celebrates with street parties held along the Amstel, Warmoesstraat and Reguliersdwarsstraat.

GRACHTENFESTIVAL

Third week in Aug Ⓦ www.grachtenfestival.nl.

International musicians perform at over ninety classical music events at historical locations around the three main canals, as well as the River Ij. Includes the Prisengracht Concert, one of the world's most prestigious concerts.

UITMARKT

Last weekend in Aug W www.uitmarkt.nl.
Every cultural organization in the city,
from opera to theatre, advertises its
forthcoming programme of events
with free preview performances held
around the Dam, Waterlooplein or
Nieuwmarkt.

OPEN MONUMENT DAY

First or second weekend in Sept W www
.openmonumentendag.nl.
For two days monuments throughout
the Netherlands that are normally
closed or have restricted opening
times throw open their doors to the
public for free.

THE JORDAAN FESTIVAL

Second or third weekend in Sept W www
.jordaanfestival.nl.
A three-day street festival in the
Jordaan. There's a commercial fair
on Palmgracht, talent contests on
Elandsgracht, a few street parties
and a culinary fair on the Sunday
afternoon at the Noordermarkt.

AMSTERDAM DANCE FESTIVAL

Late Oct W www.amsterdam-dance-event.nl.
A four-day festival, hosting hundreds
of national and international DJs
taking over all dance venues in the
city. Also a conference for turntable
professionals. Tickets for all events
have to be purchased separately and
tend to sell out quickly.

MUSEUM NIGHT

Sat in early Nov W www.n8.nl.
A great opportunity to explore
Amsterdam's museums in the wee
hours. Most museums are open

until 2am, hosting DJ performances,
workshops and concerts.

CANNABIS CUP

Late Nov W www.hightimes.com.
Five-day harvest festival with
seminars, tours and music events
held at the Nachttheater Sugar
Factory (see p.71) and the Melkweg
(see p.71), which also hosts
a competition to find the best
cultivated seed. Judging is open to
the general public.

PARADE OF SINT NICOLAAS

Second or third Sun in Nov
The traditional parade of *Sinterk-
laas* (Santa Claus) through the city
on his white horse, starting from
behind Centraal Station where
he arrives by steam boat, before
parading down the Damrak towards
Rembrandtplein. It all finishes in
Leidseplein on the balcony of the
Stadsschouwburg.

PAKJESAVOND
(PRESENT EVENING)

Dec 5
Though it tends to be a private affair,
Pakjesavond, rather than Christmas
Day, is when Dutch kids receive their
Christmas presents.

NEW YEAR'S EVE

Dec 31
Fireworks and celebrations are
everywhere, and most bars and
discos stay open until morning.
This might just qualify as the wildest
and most reckless street partying
in Europe.

Chronology

1200s > Amsterdam begins to prosper.

1425 > Digging of the Singel, Amsterdam's first horseshoe-shaped canal.

1530s > Inspired by Martin Luther and subsequently Calvin, Protestantism takes root.

1555 > Fanatically Catholic Habsburg Philip II becomes king of Spain and ruler of the Low Countries, including Amsterdam. Philip prepares to bring his heretical subjects to heel.

1566 > The Protestants strike back, purging churches of their "papist" reliquaries and shrines.

1567 > Philip dispatches a huge army to the Low Countries to suppress his religious opponents; the pre-eminent Protestant leader is William the Silent, Prince William of Orange-Nassau.

1578 > Amsterdam deserts the Spanish cause and declares for William, switching from Catholicism to Calvinism at the same time.

1579 > The seven northern provinces of the Low Countries sign the Union of Utrecht, an alliance against Spain that is the first unification of the Netherlands; the signees call themselves the United Provinces. The Spanish Netherlands (now Belgium) remain under Habsburg control.

Sixteenth century > The Golden Age. Amsterdam becomes the emporium for the products of Europe as well as the East and West Indies. By the middle of the century Amsterdam's wealth is spectacular.

1613 > Enlargement of Amsterdam begins with the three great canals of the Grachtengordel.

1648 > Peace with Spain; Dutch independence is recognized.

1672 > William III of Orange becomes ruler of the United Provinces.

1770–1790 > Amsterdam is split into two opposing factions – the Orangists (supporters of the House of Orange) and the Patriots (who are pro-French).

1795 > The French army occupies the United Provinces. Many of the Dutch elite's privileges are removed.

1814 > After Napoleon's defeat at Waterloo, Frederick William of Orange-Nassau is crowned King William I of the United Kingdom of the Netherlands, incorporating both the United Provinces and the former Spanish Netherlands. The seat of government becomes Den Haag (The Hague).

1830 > The provinces of what had been the Spanish Netherlands revolt against Frederick William and establish the separate Kingdom of Belgium. Amsterdam stagnates.

1914–18 > The Netherlands remains neutral during World War I.

1940 > In World War II, the Germans overrun the Netherlands.

1941 > The Germans start rounding up and deporting the city's Jews in earnest.

1942 > Anne Frank plus family and friends hide away in the back annexe in the Prinsengracht.

1944 > Betrayal and capture of the Franks; Anne dies in Belsen concentration camp, but her father – Otto – survives the war and publishes his daughter's diary in 1947.

May 1945 > The Allies liberate Amsterdam, but many die of starvation during the hard winter of 1945-6.

1960s > Amsterdam changes from a conservative city into a hotbed of hippy action.

1976 > The Netherlands decriminalizes (but does not legalize) the possession of soft drugs, principally cannabis. The first dope-selling "coffeeshops" open.

Late 1970s > Amsterdam's squatter movement booms.

1984 > The squatting movement has a series of major show downs with the police. There are mass riots.

Late 1980s > The squatter movement fades away.

1990s > Several huge redevelopment schemes are planned, most notably among the old docklands bordering the River IJ.

2000 > The Dutch parliament repeals the laws prohibiting brothels.

2001 > The Netherlands becomes the first country in the world to recognize gay marriages.

November 2, 2004 > Filmmaker Theo Van Gogh is shot dead in Amsterdam by Mohammed Bouyeri, a Moroccan by descent, who is enraged by Van Gogh's cinematic treatment of Islam. Across the country, race relations become tenser.

2005–6 > At a time when the country needs clear political leadership, the Rightist coalition that has a majority in the national parliament proves unstable. Immigration and race relations remain big issues.

2007–10 > The developers start rebuilding the Oosterdok, but they come a cropper with the Noord-Zuidlijn underground metro line. Costs balloon, the tunnels fill with water and the foundations of several old houses are undermined. The completion date is delayed to 2015. A sense of political disillusionment is reflected in the city elections of 2010, when much of the popular vote goes to the small parties of both the right and left.

DUTCH

It's unlikely that you'll need to speak anything other than English while you're in Amsterdam. The following Dutch words and phrases should be the most you'll need to get by, though menus are nearly always multilingual.

Words and phrases

BASICS AND GREETINGS

yes	ja
no	nee
please	alstublieft
(no) thank you	(nee) dank u or bedankt
hello	hallo or dag
good morning	goedemorgen
good afternoon	goedemiddag
good evening	goedenavond
goodbye	tot ziens
do you speak English?	spreekt u Engels?
I don't understand	Ik begrijp het niet
women/men	vrouwen/mannen
children	kinderen

NUMBERS

0	nul
1	een
2	twee
3	drie
4	vier
5	vijf
6	zes
7	zeven
8	acht
9	negen
10	tien
11	elf
12	twaalf
13	dertien
14	veertien
15	vijftien
16	zestien
17	zeventien
18	achttien
19	negentien
20	twintig
21	een en twintig
22	twee en twintig
30	dertig
40	veertig
50	vijftig
60	zestig
70	zeventig
80	tachtig
90	negentig
100	honderd
101	honderd een
1000	duizend

Food and drink

BASICS

boter	butter
boterham/broodje	sandwich/roll
brood	bread
dranken	drinks
eieren	eggs
erwtensoep/snert	pea soup with bacon or sausage
groenten	vegetables
honing	honey
hoofdgerechten	main courses
kaas	cheese
koud	cold
nagerechten	desserts
patates/frites	chips/French fries
sla/salade	salad
smeerkaas	cheese spread
stokbrood	French bread
suiker	sugar
uitsmijter	ham or cheese with eggs on bread
vis	fish
vlees	meat
voorgerechten	starters
vruchten	fruit
warm	hot
zout	salt

MEAT AND POULTRY

biefstuk (hollandse)	steak
biefstuk (duitse)	hamburger
eend	duck
fricandeau	roast pork

fricandel	frankfurter-like sausage
gehakt	minced meat
ham	ham
kalfsvlees	veal
kalkoen	turkey
karbonade	chop
kip	chicken
lamsvlees	lamb
lever	liver
spek	bacon
worst	sausages

FISH

garnalen	prawns
haring	herring
haringsalade	herring salad
kabeljauw	cod
makreel	mackerel
mosselen	mussels
oesters	oysters
paling	eel
schelvis	haddock
schol	plaice
tong	sole
zalm	salmon

VEGETABLES

aardappelen	potatoes
bloemkool	cauliflower
bonen	beans
champignons	mushrooms
erwten	peas
hutspot	mashed potatoes and carrots
knoflook	garlic
komkommer	cucumber
prei	leek
rijst	rice
sla	salad, lettuce
uien	onions
wortelen	carrots
zuurkool	sauerkraut

COOKING TERMS

belegd	filled or topped
doorbakken	well-done
gebakken	fried/baked
gebraden	roasted
gegrild	grilled
gekookt	boiled
gerookt	smoked
gestoofd	stewed
half doorbakken	medium-done
rood	rare

SWEETS AND DESSERTS

appelgebak	apple tart or cake
gebak	pastry
IJs	ice cream
koekjes	biscuits
oliebollen	doughnuts
pannekoeken	pancakes
poffertjes	small pancakes, fritters
(slag)room	(whipped) cream
speculaas	spice and honey-flavoured biscuit
stroopwafels	waffles
taai-taai	Dutch honey cake
vla	custard

DRINKS

bessenjenever	blackcurrant gin
droog	dry
frisdranken	soft drinks
jenever	Dutch gin
karnemelk	buttermilk
koffie	coffee
koffie verkeerd	coffee with warm milk
kopstoot	beer with a jenever chaser
melk	milk
pils	Dutch beer
proost!	cheers!
sinaasappelsap	orange juice
thee	tea
vruchtensap	fruit juice
wijn (wit/rood/rosé)	wine (white/red/rosé)
vieux	Dutch brandy
zoet	sweet

PUBLISHING INFORMATION

This first edition published April 2011 by **Rough Guides Ltd**

80 Strand, London WC2R 0RL

11, Community Centre, Panchsheel Park, New Delhi 110017, India

Distributed by the Penguin Group

Penguin Books Ltd, 80 Strand, London WC2R 0RL

Penguin Group (USA) 375 Hudson Street, NY 10014, USA

Penguin Group (Australia) 250 Camberwell Road, Camberwell, Victoria 3124, Australia

Penguin Group (NZ) 67 Apollo Drive, Mairangi Bay, Auckland 1310, New Zealand

Rough Guides is represented in Canada by

Tourmaline Editions Inc., 662 King Street West, Suite 304, Toronto, Ontario, M5V 1M7

Typeset in Minion and Din to an original design by Henry Iles and Dan May.

Printed and bound in China

© Martin Dunford, Phil Lee and Karoline Thomas 2011

Maps © Rough Guides

No part of this book may be reproduced in any form without permission from the publisher except for the quotation of brief passages in reviews.

148pp includes index

A catalogue record for this book is available from the British Library

ISBN 978-1-84836-235-2

The publishers and authors have done their best to ensure the accuracy and currency of all the information in **Pocket Rough Guide Amsterdam**, however, they can accept no responsibility for any loss, injury, or inconvenience sustained by any traveller as a result of information or advice contained in the guide.

1 3 5 7 9 8 6 4 2

MIX
Paper from
responsible sources
FSC www.fsc.org FSC™ C018179

ROUGH GUIDES CREDITS

Text editor: Lucy White

Layout: Ajay Verma

Cartography: Katie Lloyd-Jones

Picture editor: Mark Thomas

Photography: Roger Norum, Natascha Sturny and Mark Thomas

Proofreader: Richard Lim

Production: Rebecca Short

Cover design: Nicole Newman, Dan May and Chloë Roberts

THE AUTHORS

Martin Dunford is also the author of Rough Guides to Rome, Italy and The Netherlands, among others. One of the founding members of Rough Guides, he is now a freelance writer, editor and publishing consultant living in London and Norfolk with his wife Caroline and two daughters.

Phil Lee has been writing for Rough Guides for well over twenty years. His other books in the series include Canada, Norway, Belgium & Luxembourg, Bruges, Mallorca, England and Toronto. He lives in Nottingham, where he was born and raised.

HELP US UPDATE

We've gone to a lot of effort to ensure that the first edition of **Pocket Rough Guide Amsterdam** is accurate and up-to-date. However, things change – places get "discovered", opening hours are notoriously fickle, restaurants and rooms raise prices or lower standards. If you feel we've got it wrong or left something out, we'd like to know, and if you can remember the address, the price, the hours, the phone number, so much the better.

Please send your comments with the subject line "**Pocket Rough Guide Amsterdam Update**" to ⓔ mail@roughguides.com. We'll credit all contributions and send a copy of the next edition (or any other Rough Guide if you prefer) for the very best emails.

Find more travel information, connect with fellow travellers and book your trip on ⓦ www .roughguides.com

PHOTO CREDITS

Front cover Tulips, Bloemenmarkt © Michele Falzone
Back cover Bridge over canal © Tim Draper/ Rough Guides
p.4 Canal boat © Dave Hanson/Getty Images
p.15 Red Light District © Floris Leeuwenberg/ Corbis
p.15 Anne Frank House © Popperphoto/Corbis
p.15 Sunflowers © Van Gogh Museum
p.15 Vondel Park © Stefano Amantini/Corbis
p.15 Royal Palace © Guido Cozzi/Corbis

p.17 Amstelring © Lee Snider/Corbis
p.17 Vincent's Room © Van Gogh Museum
p.19 Brouwersgracht © Frans Lemmens/Getty
p.77 Tapas © Simon Reddy/Alamy
p.80 Rembrandthuis © Rembrandthuis Museum
p.81 Close up of Diamond © Patrick Forget/ Alamy
p.97 The Yellow House © Van Gogh Museum
p.103 Albert Cuypstraat market © Picture Contact/Alamy
p.110 Grill Plate Restaurant © Hotel Okura
p.114 Keukenhof Gardens © Bill Coster/Alamy

Index

Maps are marked in **bold**.